Fool's Gold

Searching for Goodness in the Human Heart

Cathy,
God bless you. Live well + believe in your future story.
Jim
5/24/13

Jim Ott

Fool's Gold by Jim Ott Copyright © 2013
ISBN: 978-0-9827772-9-9

All Rights Reserved

BHC PUBLISHING

Published by BHC Publishing, Dubuque, Iowa

Copyedited by Becky Barnhart

AlinaCrow

Illustrations, cover, and book design by Alina Crow

All scripture quotations, unless otherwise indicated, are taken from the Holy Bible, New International Version®, NIV®. Copyright ©1973, 1978, 1984, 2011 by Biblica, Inc.™ Used by permission of Zondervan. All rights reserved worldwide. www.zondervan.com The "NIV" and "New International Version" are trademarks registered in the United States Patent and Trademark Office by Biblica, Inc.™

Printed by Carlisle Ryan Digital Print & Services, Dubuque, Iowa

No part of this publication may be reproduced, stored in a retrieval system, or transmitted in any form or by any means, electronic, mechanical, photocopying, recording, scanning, or otherwise without prior written permission by the Publisher or Author.

For Teresa—a small offering in return for all you have sacrificed for me.

Contents

Introduction 1
Fool's Gold and Fool's Good 6
It All Began in a Garden 9
Standards 13
Consequences 27
Feeling Good vs. Being Good 32
The Should Do—Do Do Gap 37
Did Things Really Change? 43
Good God/Bad God 55
Fool's Gold Is Hard—Real Gold Is Moldable 62
Looking for Jesus in All the Wrong Places 74
The Most Important Resource? 83
Taking Sides 88
An Application from Psalm 15 101
The Fool's Road 106
You Are Going to Be Some Kind of Fool! 111
About the Author 119

Introduction

I was on vacation with my family and we were driving in the Washington, DC area on a four-lane highway when we were passed by a brand new yellow Corvette. That in itself is not unusual. I am an old guy and so I drive slowly—at least slower than a Corvette typically does! But as the nice, brand new yellow Corvette went past, I noticed that just over the word "Corvette" on the back of the car was one of those Jesus fish. It was just the normal one. It didn't have "Jesus" or "Icthus" in the middle and it wasn't one of those ones with the feet that say "Darwin." It was just a plain, silver fish on the back of a brand new yellow Corvette.

But as soon as it passed by and I had a look at the fish, I turned to my wife and said, "Now that just isn't working for me," and pointed to the Jesus fish. "What's that?" she inquired, trying hard to be interested in another of my amazingly insightful observations.

"A Jesus fish on a new yellow Corvette. Somehow, they just don't seem to go together," I replied.

"Uh-huh," my wife replied. I shook my head slowly, hoping that she understood the profound irony that I had so astutely noted. After all, would Jesus drive a Corvette?

Our trip had taken us from our home in Iowa, through Michigan for a stop at my sister's and then to Toronto, Gettysburg, and Washington, DC. Now we were heading back to Michigan where we were to attend a family wedding. Toronto was great and my son got to see the Stanley Cup at the Hockey Hall of Fame, so his trip was complete.

Visiting Gettysburg had been more challenging. We took the auto tour, which I certainly recommend. At every turn, there is another monument to a division or regiment or one of the states. As you read the history and survey the fields where thousands of men died over the course of three days, it is hard not to be moved to tears. The next day we began our time in DC and visited Arlington National Cemetery where again, the tragic toll of war is on display and one is moved to the point of tears by the ultimate sacrifice of so many in the cause of war.

Through these two days, as an American, I was moved with respect, honor and even pride. So many had given up so much defending our country and in many ways protecting the freedoms that my family and I enjoy on a daily basis with almost no sacrifice required on our part. I tried to imagine what it was like to be in the actual battles that these men fought and wondered if I would have been equal to the task even when I was young.

But in the midst of all this amazement, one question kept running through my mind as I considered the events of Gettysburg specifically and what was represented by the graves and memorials at Arlington in general. Knowing these stories, knowing what happened here, knowing why all these men died—how could anyone come to the conclusion that people are basically good?

And yet, that seems to be the prevailing view of the "nature of man" in our American culture. If I have heard it once, I've heard it a thousand times: "He is really a good person inside." This is almost always said in the context of justifying or explaining away why this "good" person just hurt someone by their actions—verbal, physical, or otherwise. Funerals are great places to hear this reasoning as well. I am not in favor of rudeness at wakes and funerals, but I have never heard someone's "goodness" questioned at their wake or funeral. Part of this is polite manners, but part is also the easy answer of our current prevailing worldview: people are basically good, even when they don't act like they are!

In this view, people are good, but are capable of doing bad things. However, the bad things occasionally done by good people do not negate the inherent goodness that is assumed as being at the core of everyone's soul. This view is found not only in the world at large but is prevalent in many if not most Christian churches as well. In some churches, the traditional biblical understanding of the sinful nature of people is taught and even affirmed, but it is not lived out in the way people actually deal with each other and with their own lives. In other churches, the biblical teaching has been lost completely and inherent goodness is assumed and taught.

But regardless of traditional biblical teachings and understandings, the idea that people are basically good seems to contradict the rules of common sense. The evidence just doesn't support the assertion. It is hard to look around at the basic state of the world in just about any area you might choose and come to the conclusion that goodness is the rule and bad things done by people are the exception. Poverty? Infant mortality and childhood disease? Hunger? Economic disparities between the rich and poor? Environmental concerns? War? Social justice? Racism? Any of the many other-isms? Freedom of speech, religion, assembly? Government corruption? Corporate greed? Can you think of more? Which of these looks to you like goodness is in charge?

A fairly recent example of human goodness was seen when Haiti experienced a horrible earthquake in January of 2010. If you go back and look at articles and internet postings from the time, you will discover a number that talk about the "human spirit" and how the response of those who donated time and money to relief efforts renewed people's faith in basic human goodness. Certainly, the response of people to those who are suffering is an example of how people can do good things. But if people are basically good in their hearts, why were people in Haiti living in the conditions they were in the first place? Why are people still living in those conditions now? If we are good, why do we allow people to live in desperate poverty?

A general survey of the state of the world, human history, or current affairs in your state and local area requires most of us to overlook the obvious in order to come to the conclusion that people are good. But it's closer to home than that. You don't have to look any further than your own thoughts and feelings to see that there is a problem. The idea that people are good doesn't even pass the test of one's own heart.

As an example, take the nice brand new yellow Corvette. When I saw that Jesus fish on the back of that Corvette, I did something with that information. I did what everyone does on some level. I took the information I had and compared it to a standard and came to the conclusion that the Jesus fish on the yellow Corvette violated that standard, thus leaving me free to judge the person who would drive a new yellow Corvette with a Jesus sticker on the back. And what was that standard? The standard was simply that I would never do that. And anyone who does something I would not do must be wrong since I am not wrong (we will deal with this later, but no one ever holds an opinion that he or she knows is wrong).

When I mentioned my wife's "Uh-huh" earlier, it was not possible to include the full non-verbal tone that it had in the car. My wife is great at identifying faulty thinking, a gift for which I am very grateful, but which has left me exposed many times. So, while I was hoping that she understood what I was saying, in truth her "Uh-huh" let me know that that I was missing something. And it's pretty simple isn't it?

The guy in the Corvette was obviously well off and my conclusion was that if you are that rich, you should be putting your money in something other than a fancy new yellow sports car and then slapping a Jesus fish on it to make you look good. My thinking was faulty in two ways. First, I don't know anything about the guy driving that Corvette and can't possibly know what he does with whatever amount of money he may or may not have.

Second, and deeper, is that compared to most people in the world, I am exactly the same as the guy in the Corvette. Most people in the world will not see in their lifetime the money I make in a year. Here I am taking two weeks to run all over the eastern part of the US and Canada, spending a couple thousand dollars on a vacation that most people in the world could not even imagine. In fact, a couple of thousand dollars is more than most people in the world live on for a year! I am driving one of the three cars owned by my family. Sure, it's a 2005 Caravan with dents, but compared to the rest of the world? There is really no difference between me and the guy with the Corvette. I hear my own voice echoing that of Jesus' disciples in Matthew 26:9 saying, "That Corvette could have been sold at a high price and the money given to the poor."

At the same time, I hear the words of Paul in Romans 2:1 saying, "You, therefore, have no excuse, you who pass judgment on someone else, for at whatever point you judge the other, you are condemning yourself, because you who pass judgment do the same things." In both cases, I am wrong even though I feel so right!

I am not good at the core of who I am. I am judgmental, among other things. And I think that this is true of every human being on earth. We simply are not good at our core. We can do good things, but those things are done in spite of the core of our being, not because of it. I don't say this to be mean or to make people feel bad, but because I believe it to be the truth and the framework that best explains why our world is the way it is and why our lives are the way they are. I also believe that a proper understanding of this view of people offers the most hope for personal and corporate salvation in all its forms.

What I hope to explore in the coming pages is that the prevailing idea that people are basically good (the rule) but that they sometimes do bad things (the exception) is in fact the opposite of what is true, even though it is what most people seem to believe. Rather, the evidence seems to indicate that people are basically bad (the rule) but they are capable of doing good and even great things (the exception). Discovering this basic truth about human nature allows us to overcome it, and allows us to be refined so that the true gold that is the value of every human being can be discovered and cherished. This process is not easy or even pleasant but the results are, well, golden!

Fool's Gold and Fool's Good

Here is an interesting story of a situation in which a major mistake was made when so-called "fool's gold" was mistaken for the real thing! (Source: http://www3.sympatico.ca/goweezer/canada/z00frob3.htm)

Martin Frobisher's Third Voyage— 1578 Gold Fever

Gold Fever had struck England. Believing she had a source of gold equal to the Spanish in South America, Queen Elizabeth I commissioned yet another voyage for Martin Frobisher. With investment backing, Frobisher set sail in 1578 with 15 ships, 300 Cornish miners, and enough lumber to build a colony. It was the largest Arctic expedition in history.

Shortly after setting sail, one of the ships deserted and returned to England. Later, before reaching Greenland, the ship carrying the lumber sank, thus ending any hope of settlement. Still, Frobisher continued where he mined 1,100 tons of ore and returned to England.

The ore, however, turned out to be worthless iron pyrite. Many of the investors went bankrupt and Frobisher's reputation was ruined. The ore Martin Frobisher brought from the Arctic remains in England today. It was used to repair the roads in the county of Kent.

For years beyond our counting, the human race has been seeking gold as a source of wealth. Prospectors around the world have sought after gold as a means to gaining a fortune. We certainly understand that gold is precious although the why may be a bit hard to understand if we actually think about it! Somewhere in the ground is this metal. If you find it, people will want it and will pay you handsomely for it. On the surface, the appeal of gold is obvious. It is pretty and can be easily formed into all kinds of beautiful objects to ornament the body or one's dwelling or a palace or wherever wealth is displayed. But if it was just that, just shiny and pretty, other things would do just as well.

That's where fool's gold comes in. Fool's gold is a substance called pyrite. I am by no means an expert on minerals, but just a little passing research on pyrite leads to a couple of discoveries. First, it is very common. It is also easy to spot because it's already shiny. It is often gold colored. If the only appeal of real gold were that it was shiny, many fools would have become rich with shiny pyrite! Pyrite is everywhere. But the appeal of gold is much deeper than what it looks like when it is in its finished product. (Why gold and not any of the elements we find in the world? For an easy to follow and fun treatment of this, I encourage the reader to check out a story that aired on NPR in November of 2010: A Chemist Explains Why Gold Beat Out Lithium, Osmium, Einsteinium . . ." {www.npr.org/templates/transcript/transcript.php?storyId=131430755})

I want to emphasize that I believe that people are the most valuable thing on earth. There is nothing more valuable than a human soul. A single human life is more valuable than all the gold on the planet. My belief rests on the price that was paid for individual human souls in the form of the sacrifice of Jesus. I also want to emphasize that I love people. I like being around them and meeting new people and finding out how they think. (In the midst of that statement, I also have to confess that when I first meet a person, my natural instinct is to figure out what's wrong with them! I have to work against that all the time.) However, I also believe that people are not inherently good, only that they are inherently valuable. We make a mistake that leads to frustration and disappointment when we look at the shiny things on the surface of people's behavior and assume that they are good all the way through. This is "fool's good."

Even a large nugget of real gold is of limited use until it is refined, purified, and molded into a presentable form. People are the same way. Good deeds are common and even desired, but they are not evidence of inner goodness. Similarly, bad deeds are common and not desired, but they are not evidence of a person of no value. What lies at the core of people is a value that is beyond even our vain imaginations! But like gold embedded in a lot of muck, our inner value has been embedded in brokenness and self-centeredness. The true value of the human soul can only be found through a refining process that purges all the impurities that have surrounded and corrupted our true value and which leads to us being formed into a presentable form that reflects the inner value. This is a lifetime process and is really never completed because of the nature of the impurities that cannot be fully removed as long as we live in this fallen world. In the meantime, by submitting to the refining process and having a realistic view of the nature of people, we can make our lives and this world a little bit more like the garden where it all started.

It All Began in a Garden

My son has a paper route and I get up early to help him, as much because it's good for me to get the exercise as because he needs the help. One of the houses on the route has a front porch where we put the paper in the front door. Next to the steps to the front porch is a gate that leads to a garden area on the side of the house. There is a variety of plants and little walks and a patio area with a table and chairs. It is one of the prettiest places on the whole paper route. A sign on the gate says, "It all began in a garden."

This house is also the least favorite of ours on the route. If you have ever had a paper route or your children have, I'll bet you can guess why. Dogs. BIG dogs! There are two of them and if they are out in the garden area when we arrive to deliver the papers, they both bark with what seems like a serious desire to take something out of our legs! And one of the dogs—the really big one—comes right to the gate and barks and shows his teeth and seems like he is going to come right over the gate and kill us! We do our best to sneak on to the porch and get the paper into the door without disturbing the dogs. But when they are out and come to the gate barking, it scares the heck out of both of us! Sometimes we don't even try to get on the porch and just throw the paper in the direction of the door and run! One thing is for sure—whether or not those dogs are out, I will NEVER go into that garden no matter how beautiful it may look from outside the gate!

It's a nice picture of the biblical story in Genesis of the first garden. This is not the place to debate whether or not the Genesis account in chapters 2 and 3 is literal or figurative. For the purposes of our consideration, the point of the story is not historical accuracy but to explain why people are the way they are. It sets the stage for the rest of the Bible by explaining the problem. And the problem is this: people were walking intimately with God and lacked nothing. Life was indeed paradise when we lived in the garden. But people decided that they didn't need to do what God said but could make their own decisions. They broke fellowship with God as the source of truth and began to determine truth on their own. And it's pretty much been downhill ever since then!

In the Genesis story (chapters 2 and 3), Adam and Eve are given everything they need, and only one rule to follow: don't eat from the tree of the knowledge of good and evil. On the day that you do, God said, "You will surely die." Eat from all the other trees, but not that one. The devil comes in the form of a serpent and plants seeds of doubt in the minds of Adam and Eve. "You will not surely die," says the serpent. God doesn't want you to eat from that tree because on the day that you do, "you will be like God, knowing good and evil."

Adam and Eve go for the bait and eat from the tree and immediately think they know something. In fact, ever since that time, people have thought they knew something. People have believed that their opinions actually matter and have merit in determining truth. What used to be and still should be the exclusive arena of God (knowing what is truly good and what is truly evil) is now an arena in which people, with all our limitations of vision and knowledge, now play freely—to the great despair of all of us. We engage in continuous judgment of right and wrong in the behaviors and opinions of others and justify our actions, thoughts, and treatment of others based on those judgments. Because we don't need God to tell us what is right and wrong any more, we assume that our opinions, many strongly held, must be accurate!

This foundational assumption, that our opinion has merit in determining truth and lie, right and wrong, good and evil, is so deeply laid that most of the time, if not all of the time, we are not even aware that it is present and active in our thinking. It is a foundation that was laid at the moment that people decided that they did not need God to determine good and evil, but that they could "do it themselves," to paraphrase pretty much every two or three year old on the planet!

The Genesis story presents the problem as being that people have, in fact, become like God in terms of determining what is good and evil. It's just that people are not very good at it. And every human conflict can be boiled down to this basic idea—we all think we are right and when two of us see things differently, one of us must admit that he/she is wrong or we must fight or at the very least ignore each other.

Before Adam and Eve took the "Big Bite," the standard of good and evil was God. All decisions and thoughts and opinions were measured against what God said was right and wrong and there was no debate. If there was ever a question about this, apparently Adam and Eve could just ask God since the relationship between people and God at that point in the story was so intimate that God walked and talked with Adam in the garden (Genesis 3:8). But as soon as the first bite of knowledge of good and evil was taken, people began to have another standard: the standard of personal opinion.

"Hey, we are buck naked here. We better get some clothes on!"
To which God said, "Who told you that you were naked?"

It's not that being naked was the issue. The real issue is that prior to the Big Bite, it wasn't wrong to be naked. With this new knowledge, suddenly people reached a conclusion that was not of God's making: being naked is wrong. People have been trying to cover up ever since, literally and figuratively—perhaps because our greatest fear is being exposed.

Suddenly, there was a new standard and the intimacy with God was no longer present. God had to run the people out of the garden and post an angel with a flaming sword to guard it so they couldn't get back in. I kind of get this because of those dogs on the paper route. The garden is beautiful, but I can't go in!

So now, we are left with this deep foundation of the knowledge of good and evil. We develop our own standards of right and wrong and measure others by them. This happens at the individual relationship level all the way up to the governmental and world religion level. And it's a mess! That's the Genesis worldview, the Big Bite Theory, if you will. It is an explanation of why people are the way they are and it gives us some clues of what we can do about it.

Standards

I am a school psychologist by trade and one of the big trends in education these days is toward standards based education. In general, this means that there are certain things a student needs to know and a student's success or failure is measured by what they know compared to that standard. This makes sense on the surface of things. We can clearly see that it is impossible to judge whether a person has succeeded or achieved unless we have a way to measure that, and measurement requires standards and tools with which to measure. These tools are of little value unless they are consistent with other tools that measure the same thing.

This is where broader standards have entered the educational system. In the old days, at least the old days of which I was a part, there were standards. However, the standards were determined more by the teacher or sometimes the school or even school district. We got grades based on how well we measured up to a certain teacher's expectations. Some teachers wanted us to show all our work and we got better grades if we showed all our work even if we didn't always understand the work we were showing! Some teachers valued class participation so we raised our hands more in that teacher's class. Some teachers just wanted good performance on the test—"Show me what you know"—so we memorized a ton of information to do well on the tests. Maybe you have a certain teacher whose standards you learned, or maybe never did! The point is that we had to measure up to the teacher's standard to get the grades.

In our current time, there has been recognition that schools are getting different results when the students are measured by the same standards (think standardized bubble sheet tests as an example). Big picture thinkers have the idea that if everyone, right down to the individual classroom teacher, was accountable for teaching the same standard in terms of content, the result would be more consistent and successful achievement across schools, districts, and even to the national level. But in order for this to happen, the standards have to be defined to the minutia of what content will be taught and what knowledge will be expected to be attained by every student. I will say as a person who has been in the education system for more than a quarter of a century, I have some problems with this universal standards approach. But intuitively, it makes sense to us! By having the same standards and measuring everyone by those standards, we will be better able to tell how students are doing, and in the optimistic version of the story, help those students who are having difficulty "measuring up." In this approach it is kind of like measuring weight—everyone on the same scale and ranked accordingly. Those who are not heavy enough get intervention and are monitored by a consistent scale that does not change and remains completely objective. The same thing happens for those who are too heavy. The goal is an acceptable weight for everyone according to a standard that everyone agrees on and is measured consistently.

So here's the thing—teachers and schools that are already doing things which allow their students to meet the standards really don't have anything to worry about in this new approach, although they may worry themselves sick anyway! It's the schools and teachers whose students are not measuring up that will be most impacted by these standards. And when that happens, the cry will immediately go up, "That's not fair!" In many cases, I would happen to agree that it isn't fair. There are so many factors that go into a student's achievement that a school simply cannot control. However, for the sake of example, consider the dynamic. When schools and teachers are not measuring up to some standard, the first response is typically to say on some level that the standard is wrong. "You don't understand our situation or our population or our unique setting. We are doing the best we can with what we have but the standard is wrong. If you changed the standard to better reflect what we deal with on a daily basis, we would do fine." In other words, we don't need to change; the standard needs to change.

Now I want to take a minute to clarify something. I am using this example as a picture of a concept about standards in general and how people deal with them. There are many schools and teachers that are working hard to improve the education that students are receiving, some to the point of revamping their whole system and approach to teaching and meeting the needs of the students. The point of the illustration is to say these two things:

1. People want and expect there to be a standard and want to be successful in meeting that standard.
2. When confronted with a standard that people can't meet or aren't meeting, the normal reaction is:
   a. to appeal for a change in the standard (if I am the one who can't meet the standard), or
   b. to appeal for a change in behavior (if others aren't meeting my standard).

The story in Genesis has another part that takes place before the whole garden mess. According to the account, people were created "in the image of God." Now it should be fairly clear that this does not mean that people were created to look like God. A better understanding is that unlike the other living things in the world, we were given aspects of God's character and thought processes. Animals, especially when left alone by people, do what they were created to do and they don't deviate from that. Birds are birds and don't try to do anything else, nor would it ever occur to them that they could or should. They are limited in their ability to think beyond themselves. Even many of the fascinating things that are being discovered about what higher primates are capable of in terms of communication are only being discovered in controlled settings manipulated by people. No gorilla ever asked if he could be taken out of his natural environment and put in a confined area in some zoo or lab so that he could get in on some of those cool experiments they are doing with sign language. Left to himself, a gorilla will just do what gorillas have always done. He doesn't aspire to something else. He does what his created nature leads him to do.

One aspect of thinking that is not viewed in other animals in the same way as it is seen in people is the issue of motivation, especially as it relates to good and evil. For example, watch any nature show involving animals eating other animals. The images will be gruesome to watch at times. But regardless of whether the show is being produced from a creationist or evolutionist perspective, you will never hear the narrator say anything like, "That poor baby antelope! Those tigers are so cruel and mean. They clearly lack any kind of positive moral fiber. It just isn't fair that the tigers use their superior speed and strength to abuse those poor baby antelope." Instead, if the nature program is from an evolutionary point of view there will be commentary about survival of the fittest and making the herd stronger by weeding out the weaker members and such. If it is from a creationist point of view, the commentary will be along the lines of the consequences of the fall and of animals simply doing what they were created to do. In neither case will there be a moral judgment of the animal behavior.

But watch any television show about people, documentary or dramatic, and the content is almost always about the morality of the people and the situation. Judgment on the part of the viewer is assumed. While the show may or may not be trying to manipulate that judgment in one way or another, the fact the viewers are judging is unquestioned. Once again, it won't matter if the show is being told from a faith based or purely secular point of view. We may not agree on how we got to this place of judgment, but everyone knows that human beings are moral creatures and that we are obsessed with the issue of fairness and with being "right."

You don't have to watch a television show to see that this issue of fairness is at the core of human existence. If you have small children, even down to three and four, try this experiment at home. Tell the kids you are going to have some ice cream. Then give one of the children an extra-large bowl heaping with ice cream and the other child or children one small scoop in a smaller bowl. See how that works out for you! At a very early age, children are already comparing themselves with others and invoking a standard of "fairness" that they expect to be followed. When it is not followed to their satisfaction? Well, if you have had children, you know the result. And if you don't have children, I'll bet you can guess.

It would be great if we got over this childhood fixation on fairness, but our political conversations in our country clearly indicate that we don't. Listen to current politicians and political commentators and imagine that they are four year olds arguing over a bowl of ice cream. Pretty quickly, it is apparent that both sides of an argument are saying the same basic thing: I have a standard of fairness that is not being met and if the other side would meet my standard, everything would be okay. Of course, politicians are better at disguising that they are mostly interested in their own bowl of ice cream. They talk about representing the people, or the oppressed, or the good of the country, or whatever. But while the complexity of the argument has changed, the foundation has not. People want and expect there to be a standard and when that standard is not met, they expect others to change to meet the standard, or they expect others to change the standard so that they do not have to change.

What we call "fairness" at the childhood level gets a name change in the adult world. We refer to it as "justice." But it's the same thing in new clothes. At the core of all human beings is a desire for things to be the way they think they should be in terms of each one's standard of fairness or justice. Even with people who seemingly have no conscience (think sociopathic serial killers), they really believe that what they are doing is acceptable according to their version of right and wrong.

This deep, abiding desire for justice is part of what it means to be created in the image of God. God sees everything from his perspective of justice and evaluates behavior based on that. We do the same thing. The difference is that by definition, God's standard of justice is 100% correct at all times. Before the Big Bite in the garden, according to the message of the Genesis story, people simply followed God's standard and there were no problems. But as soon as we took a bite of that fruit, we thought we knew something and began to see justice through our own eyes. The desire for justice and morality and fairness is a God given part of who we are. It mirrors God's own desires, his character. But our interpretation has been corrupted by our mistaken belief that we don't need an external standard given from God. We can do it ourselves! And the more we do it ourselves, the more we drift from the original standard to one that is more selfish, self-absorbed, and self-justifying.

For many people, this is an obvious and well-known concept. But I am not sure that even those of us who subscribe to a biblical worldview about the nature of people understand how much this distorted sense of fairness based on our own opinion is a part of everything we think and do. Every time you meet a new person and form an opinion of them, you are dealing with a piece of that Big Bite lodged in your throat. Every time you get angry at some situation you read about in the newspaper, you are dealing with your own personal, deep-seated knowledge of good and evil. Every time you curse the stupid driver who just interfered with your commute, you are sitting in the place of judgment reserved only for God. *Every* time. There are no exceptions to when this foundational basis of our brokenness is in operation.

As another example, if you have ever served on a committee or board at a church where there has ever been a disagreement on some issue (maybe this doesn't happen at your church!), you have seen this principle of personal standards and fairness in play. Everyone who has an opinion about the matter being considered wants there to be a standard and expects it to be met. But even though there are well-intentioned followers of Jesus around the table, there seems to be different standards at work based on the opinions of those who are involved in the disagreement. I am sorry to say that I have been a part of many of these situations in my own church and if you have also, you know that emotions can run pretty high when this collision of standards takes place. But in the midst of these "discussions," I have never once heard anyone, including me, say, "You know, this is really about the tree of good and evil. Every one of us here actually thinks we know something and that our opinion must be right because we hold it so strongly. We are all looking for justice and fairness that really only God can define." Instead, what I do hear is layer upon layer of intellectual and even emotional justification of why each individual's standard is correct. It becomes all about defending our personal standard when the real problem is that we think that we have a right to define the standard in the first place. The problem is so much deeper than the content of the argument and it all goes back to the garden.

People, having been created in the image of God, have the ability to think beyond their animal instincts—to engage in metacognition—thinking about one's thinking. People have been created with a desire for a standard of justice that is a part of the character of God. In our rejection of God as the source of that standard, we have set up our own standards that in many cases are different than God's and in almost all cases are different from those of other people. To be sure, we tend to align ourselves with others who have similar standards. Examples range from political parties to denominations to issue-oriented groups such as People for the Ethical Treatment of Animals and Right to Life. But as any of us know who are involved in any group, there are differences of standards between individuals even within these groups (we will deal with this more later). With teenagers, this aligning with people of similar standards is called "peer pressure" and we encourage teens not to do it. As adults, we call it "activism" or "being involved" and we encourage it. Regardless, the foundation is the same. We are looking for people whose standard is relatively similar to ours so that we can feel justified in our opinions. The problem is at the foundation, not in the actions and opinions built on that foundation.

Speaking of teenagers, I have been involved in a lot of youth ministry through the years in addition to my ongoing work as a school psychologist. So, I feel somewhat confident in saying that if you want to see the development of the individual standard problem as defined by the Genesis story, hanging out with teenagers is a good place to do that. If teenagers are young adults, then adults are just old teenagers. We get better at masking and justifying what teenagers are just coming to grips with as they develop an ever-increasing ability to think more abstractly.

Young children are primarily concerned with "It's not fair" as a general concept. But teenagers begin to understand that there is a standard involved and they expect consistency in the application of the standard. They also begin to see that they have a standard that is different from others. So, if the cry of the child is "It's not fair," the added cry of the teenager might be summed up, as "You don't understand me." (We keep "It's not fair" forever!)

I was doing some youth work through my church once and had a group discussion going on the topic of why the high school students in the group should not drink alcohol. Basically, I wanted them to move away from the worldly approach of addressing this issue, which encourages listing pros and cons and then making a good choice (a detailed look at this is coming later), and instead to look at a biblical answer they could have confidence in. As we went along, I got to the big punch line, which is contained in 1 Peter 2:13: "Submit yourselves for the Lord's sake to every authority instituted among men."

I self-righteously declared (I was pretty self-righteous in those days. Now I am just sort of self-righteous!) "The biggest reason that you should not drink is because it is against the law and the bible teaches that you should submit to the governing authorities, unless of course the governing authorities are requiring you to do something immoral or against God's word."

Immediately a girl named Jolene put her hand up and said, "You mean that you never speed?"

I paused, thought for minute, and replied in the only way that I could: "Not anymore." Dang teenagers anyway! As they begin to explore the standards in their lives, they are particularly attuned to inconsistencies in how they are applied and are often not afraid to say so.

But teenagers are also beginning to be aware that they have the ability to form their own standards that are different from those of their parents, teachers, church leaders, and even their friends. They begin to question the standards that they may have been living by but that were more or less imposed on them by others. Suddenly it's not only about how much ice cream each person gets. Now it's about whether we should eat ice cream at all (I don't think we should eat ice cream because it's not good for our health). Or maybe it's about the brand of ice cream (Are they a green company?). Or maybe it's about the flavor? (Why don't you ever buy the kind of ice cream I like?) Or perhaps it's about choice (Why do we have to have ice cream all the time? Why can't we have something else?) Teenagers are beginning to stretch their "standard" muscles in ways that are awkward to us adults only because they are so much less subtle at it than we are as full-grown adults. But we do the same things, don't we?

I used to do a talk for adults working with children entitled, "Why do you speed?" It really was all Jolene's fault. The overall point of the talk was that if you are going to be in a position of enforcing rules that some of the children or teens you are working with don't want to follow or maybe don't think are important, you have to look at your own reaction to rules that fall in the same category for you. Here were some of the things that I included in the talk based on excuses I had heard from adults through the years. See how these excuses line up with what we all do to justify why we don't live up to standards.

1. **"I don't usually go that fast" (The accidental exception)**—A nice lady came into my office one morning telling her harrowing tale of having been pulled over by the police for speeding. She said, "But I just told him, 'Officer, I don't usually go that fast. I guess I just wasn't paying attention.'" She was quite gratified that he only gave her a warning and seemed to think that her excuse was perfectly legitimate. What was amazing to me was that I knew she usually DID go that fast! And she still seemed to think she was good when she pulled this excuse out.

2. **It was a special situation. (The justified exception)**—This one is used less frequently in the world of speeding but all the time in the world of violating standards. "I was late for an important appointment so I had to speed this time." "My child was sick and I needed to hurry home and get him to the doctor." "The game was starting at 4:30 and I'm the coach so I had to

get there on time." We are especially adept at using this excuse when we violate our own standards!

3. **The other traffic moves so fast that I have to speed just to avoid getting run over!—(Everyone else is doing it.)**—Enough said on this one. Justifying our behavior based on the behavior of others just doesn't seem like a good place to be, especially if you are going to be working with kids!

4. **The speed limit doesn't make sense for this part of the road. (The standard is wrong.)**—And if I don't agree with the standard, I am free to ignore it and instead follow my own standard.

5. **There are no cops around here. (If the enforcer is not present, the standard is not in effect.)**—A variation of "It's only a crime if you get caught." The standard of behavior now becomes what you want to do in light of the authority that is present. Hardly a good message for kids who you want to follow your rules and make good decisions in their future lives!

6. **I have a lead foot. (I have a personal failing that makes it impossible for me to obey the standard.)**—In my view, this one is probably the closest to the truth in that it acknowledges that the standard was violated. But we hear this one in all kinds of ways to justify behaviors. It starts with "I'm just the kind of person who . . ." or "I can't help it . . ." and is followed with things like "I have a sweet tooth," or "I just really like beer," or "I have a fatal flaw when it comes to Italian men." Or whatever. Somehow, we are able to make a choice we made not our fault because we couldn't help it even though we were the ones who did it!

7. **Why aren't you out catching real criminals? (My violation is nothing compared to what other people are doing.)**—This involves ranking standards according to perceived importance and then deciding that there is a cut off where we no longer really have to follow the standard because we are taking care of things that are more important. This is where we find the

category of office supplies finding their way from our places of employment into our homes but not calling it "stealing."

8. **I didn't see the sign. OR My speedometer must be broken (The lie)**—We are so good at this one that we believe it ourselves a lot of the time!

I'm sure you get the picture by now. Pick your favorite area of standard violation in other people and you will quickly see that the excuses used to justify the violations fall in categories such as these. The foundational concept is that "I couldn't possibly be wrong and even if I am, it's either not my fault or else there is a good reason." (There's that "g" word again.)

Here is the big problem with standards that force us to confront the issue of what is really good and what is "fool's good." And it is related to the list of excuses above. Just like speed limit signs, we all have moral limit signs that reside within us. Favorite phrases in discussions about beliefs and morals and ethics are "What I think is . . ." or "I have always believed that . . ." or "I'm one of those people who just believe that. . . ." People do not want to be held accountable to the standards of others ("That might work for you, but I believe . . .") and the idea of absolute values that apply to all people at all times in all places has become increasingly offensive or even foreign. Discussions about "God" use the same kind of "I believe" language and the cultural norm ends up being that each person should be permitted to live by his or her own standards, beliefs, or "God."

This actually sounds really nice and in our relativistic world, it works pretty well. The big problem is when it comes to defining good and evil. Because the truth is that while all of us have internal standards that may or may not agree with others, **none of us can live up to our own standards!** Forget about God; I can't even do what *I* say is right, at least not all the time. An obvious example? I have yet to meet a person who holds lying as an internal moral good; who thinks that lying is the right thing to do. I have also yet to meet a person who hasn't told a lie. So why do people lie? The same reasons we speed.

This should not be news to anyone who has been alive longer than about 10 years. But it has huge implications for our understanding the goodness of people. If we have standards by which we decide whether people are doing the right or wrong thing, and if we are good people, why do we continually violate those standards? Why can't a person control his/her anger, or drinking, or internet wandering to pornographic sites, or hatred or daily judgment of others who violate that person's standards?

My contention is that it is because we are flawed at the core and that the "good deeds" we display are fool's good and not a valid way to define our inner self. The conflict that occurs between our beliefs about goodness and our actual behavior even at the thought level causes what we psychologists call cognitive dissonance and can result in all kinds of stress related problems including depression. To compensate for the problem, we like to find others who violate standards at extreme levels so that we can say that, "At least we are not like them." Let's take an example from the local newspaper.

Recently, a local elementary principal was let go from his employment when it was discovered that he had child pornography on his computer and that he had placed a hidden camera in the boy's bathroom at his school (I wish I was making this up.). This was on the heels of an incident within the last two school years in which an assistant principal at one of the high schools had really inappropriate contact with a female high school student in his own house where he lived with his wife and kids. The community reaction to these two incidents was predictable. People were outraged and wondered how this could ever happen. They saw these men as very sick and justifiably wanted them removed as far as possible from any children anywhere. There was a great deal of sadness that this occurred. In my own church, the pastor prayed for the men and the school staffs and parents who were directly affected.

Here's the problem: the behavior of these men is assumed to reflect an inner character deficit and their inner character is judged by the surface behavior. These are bad men and we know they are bad men because they did bad things. The rest of us feel better about our goodness because we do not do these bad things. We judge our character and the character of others based on the surface behavior of not doing bad things, which quickly translates to, "We do good things," therefore, we are good people.

In a broader context, the great Christian apologist, Ravi Zacharias, makes this obvious but needed point about comparative religions. The current worldview is that while religions may appear to be different on the surface, they are really all the same at their core. Mr. Zacharias says that the opposite is true: world religions are similar at the surface but at their core, they are dramatically and irreconcilably different. People want the easy way and so choose the former view to avoid conflict and promote the one world religion, which is tolerance.

I think we do a version of the same thing with moral character of individuals. In our desire to see goodness in the general population and especially in ourselves, we look at the surface behavior of others as evidence of deviance and see them as different when at the core we are really all the same.

Back to the principals. I completely agree that these men should not be working with children. But I assure you that virtually every man working within the school system has struggled with lust at some level. Almost all are able to keep it in check in terms of outward behavior. But almost all have had to struggle with the issue. If we were to eliminate from the school system every man who has struggled with temptations, there would be no men working in the school system at all. While these principals violated the law as well as basic morality, it began with a temptation "that is common to man" (1 Corinthians 10:13). In behavior, there is a huge difference between these men and me. In inner goodness and character, there is very little if any. The principal's bad behavior is fool's dirt and my good behavior is fool's good. It has no real meaning in terms of what is really within the human soul at the core of one's being. We comfort ourselves in our goodness and the goodness of most people by judging that these men are different than we are.

The problem is that ever since Adam and Eve ate that apple, we as people think we know something. We think we know what good and evil are and our judgments about good and evil have created problems ever since. These judgments have led to brokenness from the individual and family level all the way to the national and global level. The result is places like Gettysburg and Arlington National Cemetery and the inescapable conclusion that we are not good people—in spite of our opinions to the contrary.

Consequences

This is a topic that writes itself once a person begins to see the nature of man as being flawed, broken, and even "bad." But I think it's worth looking at the application of this concept to real life as a way to begin considering how knowing that people are not good can actually be helpful. For example, let's look at how we deal with our children!

What happens if a person subscribes to the view that people are good and then has to apply that to their own child? Recently, I was at a family camp and there was a sidewalk section where both people and bicycles were moving back and forth, as they moved between activities. One little boy, around 6 or 7, was with his mother walking when some of his friends went by on bicycles. The little boy began to run after his friends. The boy's mother was not happy with this choice as she was concerned with the safety of her son. As he continued to run, she shouted after him:

> *"I don't want you to run."*
> *"You don't want to get hit by a bicycle."*
> *"You can't run after those bikes."*
> *"You're going to get hurt."*

Can you see the pattern in the attempts to get the boy to change his behavior? As a school psychologist, I see this kind of parenting all the time. It is loaded with assumptions that the parent is not even aware she is making. Look at the comments along with the assumptions that underlie them:

Statement	Assumption
"I don't want you to run."	You want to do what I want.
"You don't want to get hit by a bicycle."	You are motivated by the same thing that motivates me.
"You can't run after those bikes."	You understand and want to follow the same interpretation of the rules that I have.
"You're going to get hurt."	Getting hurt is more important to you at this moment than catching up with your friends.

Ask yourself the obvious question: Do any of these assumptions make sense in light of what is going on in the head of a six year old?

The problem with parenting from a point of view that says that people are basically good is that it assumes that your children are good and therefore are inclined to do good things. Since you, as parent, have (a false) knowledge of what is good and what is evil, your children should be inclined to do what you would want them to do. When your children don't do what you want them to do, you as the parent begin to appeal to the inner standard that you hold, assuming that since it's a "good" standard, your kids have the same standard. And amazingly, you as the parent, appeal to that standard in some kind of indirect, vague, intellectual way as if the kid is going to stop running after the bikes and turn and say to you, "You are right mother. I hadn't really considered the risks involved with my behavior and how my behavior was violating my larger priorities of personal safety and appropriate behavior in the public eye."

The larger problem with parenting from a people-are-good perspective is that kids are going to misbehave and demonstrate selfish and even defiant behaviors at times. If a parent's underlying belief is that people are basically good, the parent is going to have to reconcile the child's difficult behavior in some other way than accepting that human nature indicates that people including one's own children are inclined to be selfish and even "bad."

The two most prevalent explanations that I encounter are that the parent begins to wonder if there is something wrong with their child or the parent begins to believe the child is being bad to get at the parent personally. This becomes very painful for parents who are left with all kinds of questions about their own effectiveness and the implications of possible deviance in their child. Because "if children are born good and my child is not, I must have done this to him."

In this area, the Big Bite Theory becomes very helpful. If one understands that children are born with a natural bent toward selfishness and rebellion and defiance then you are not surprised when all of a sudden your two-year-old looks you in the eye and says, "NO!" Instead, you roll up your sleeves and you say, "Ok, we've been waiting for this. Let's get busy." Now your role as a parent isn't to take something good and let it become what it will. Instead, your role as a parent is to begin the purification process by which the dirt that surrounds the nugget of gold that is your child's soul is removed bit my bit. Purification is not a pleasant process. For gold, it requires fire. For kids, it requires consistent discipline that provides limits around a child while he learns to keep his own "evil" in check. The bible says:

"Folly is bound up in the heart of a child, but the rod of discipline will drive it from him."—Proverbs 22:15

Another good proverb is 13:24—"Whoever spares the rod hates his child; but whoever loves him is careful to discipline him."

People really don't like these proverbs because of the emotions and opinions associated with corporal punishment and I get that. Professionally, I have encountered many children who have experienced corporal punishment that was not motivated by love with devastating consequences. I am not opposed to corporal punishment properly used but also have some fairly firm opinions regarding the conditions under which it can be effective.

But rather than debate whether or not it ought to be a literal rod let's consider the perspective from which these proverbs come. If the prevailing view of the goodness of people is true, the fool's good perspective, then children are born inclined toward good and the fact that so many of them end up not as good as they were born can only mean that the parents/environment/culture has corrupted their natural goodness.

But if the Genesis story is a better picture of the problem, then children are born with an inclination toward prideful, self-gratifying thoughts and action that will necessarily run contrary to appropriate behavior desired by the parents and the culture at large. If the adults closest to those children, in other words their parents, do not work hard to put limits on the children's natural tendencies, the children will have difficulty ever learning to have internal checks on their impulses.

We had a family attend our church for a few weeks. At one point, their son was being dropped off in the nursery and the nursery worker apparently made the mistake of using a bad word in the parent's presence—she actually said "No" to one of the children! The parents informed the nursery worker that she was not to use the word "No" with their son because they are not going to use that word with him. He was about two. All I can say to that is "Good luck!" I almost wish they had stayed around so that I knew the outcome of the story. But I can almost guarantee that one of two things happened. Either that kid is a very challenging individual to be around or those parents started saying "No!"

This is not a parenting book but here is one word of parenting advice from someone who has been in the game for a while. Learn to use the word "No" and its companions early and efficiently. And when you use the word "No" be prepared to enforce it by whatever means necessary. All you have to do is go shopping at Wal-Mart once or twice to know that for many kids the word "No" really means, "Scream louder until you get what you want."

This is what the bible is talking about when it encourages discipline with children. The Genesis story lets us know the problem. Proverbs like the ones above let us know that our part in addressing the problem starts at birth with the children who are born to us. Seeing the world in this way gives parents permission to accept that their kids are going to be challenging, defiant, and uncooperative without taking it personally.

One specific consequence of thinking that people are basically good is that parenting suffers and with it, the opportunity children have to learn to develop internal checks on their natural tendency toward self-absorption. Our American culture has taken many of the limits off of our children and we seem to be reaping the benefit of that in our day. Children make a lot of their decisions about what they want based on how it makes them feel. If it feels good, it must be good and if it doesn't feel good, don't do it. This kind of emotion based decision-making is a prescription for children becoming adults who live moment to moment based on feelings of happiness and as a result have difficulty with stability and commitment in relationships, education, and employment among other things. Let's consider this issue of feelings as it relates to goodness and what happens with our decision-making when we focus on our feelings.

Feeling Good vs. Being Good

When we took a bite of that fruit in the garden, the result was that we now know good and evil—or at least we think we do. However, because we are very emotional beings, we have confused being good with feeling good. At a very deep level, deeper than most of us are even aware of, we are convinced that what we believe is right and good. Therefore, anything that resonates with what we believe must also be right and good. Because we are easily swayed by emotion, we start to get mixed up at a chicken and egg level regarding things that make us feel good and we start to form opinions about what IS good based on what FEELS good. I know this is a repetitive paragraph but I believe that this is important and foundational for understanding the fool's good concept and how it impacts our thinking.

The easiest place for us to see this dynamic is in the area of love. At almost every Christian church wedding one goes to, the love chapter from 1 Corinthians 13 will be read in part or in whole. Weddings are emotional events and they are presumably all about love so this reading makes some sense. Here is a portion (vs. 4–8a):

> *"Love is patient, love is kind, it does not boast, it does not envy, it is not proud. It is not rude, it is not self-seeking, it is not easily angered, it keeps no record of wrongs. Love does not rejoice with evil but rejoices with the truth. It always protects, always trusts, always hopes, always perseveres. Love never fails."*

Brings a tear to your eye just reading it doesn't it? I read this at a wedding at which I was speaking recently and tried as hard as I could to make this point: There is nothing emotional about this kind of love. Emotional love is not patient and is frequently self-seeking. Emotional love is easily offended (angered) and often not very trusting. Emotional love comes and goes and anyone who has managed to stay married past the seven-year itch and on in to the 10s and 20s of years, an increasingly rare feat, will tell you that emotional love will simply not be the glue that holds it all together. Rather, 1 Corinthians 13 love is about a decision to love in spite of the ebb and flow of emotion—to love anyway, to love no matter what. It's a decision to love even when you come to the amazing discovery that this person you committed your life to is not so "good" after all!

I was at another wedding with my oldest daughter who was 21 at the time. It was a traditional wedding in a traditional church setting. In fact, the bride had wedding pictures going back three generations of family members who had been married in this same small church. After the wedding, my daughter observed that the traditional wedding ceremony is really a somewhat solemn affair; that there is almost a sense of mourning and loss. As we talked about it we wondered if that is not in fact true, that in a traditional understanding of marriage, there is a real sacrifice in the commitment being made. The bride and groom are saying, "No longer will I be able to follow my feelings in romantic relationships now that I have given myself to this one person." The traditional wedding ceremony certainly goes back to a time when there was a more prevalent belief in the brokenness of people. Maybe that ceremony came about through an understanding of something our culture has lost.

Here's what we know: in our world today, a good reason for getting a divorce is, "We just don't love each other anymore." What is that all about? In a nutshell, it's about emotional commitment. If a couple doesn't "feel" it anymore, then they should go their separate ways and find new partners with whom they do feel it. It's junior and senior high school dating carried into adulthood and what are supposed to be "adult" relationships. At one point in our country's history, a divorce was only granted based on some evidence that the commitment had been broken and often that evidence had to be of infidelity. It began to change and, as is often the case in our world, the celebrities led the way with what you may remember as the stated cause of their divorces: "Irreconcilable differences."

Obviously, as a school psychologist, this dynamic of easy, no-fault divorce has a direct impact on my work with children. In the midst of a divorce process, one or both parents will tell me, "We only want what is best for the children." And I want to say, "You mean after your own emotional wants are taken care of and you abandon your wedding vows!" But at that point, I am back to the premise of this book, which is that I am judgmental because I have a tendency to see every situation through my own definitions of what is good and evil!

The point of all of this is that in this game of defining good and evil, we often get what feels good mixed up with what is good. More accurately, we get them out of order. We seek emotional feelings and then define intellectually as good what makes us feel good instead of intellectually defining what is good and then dealing with the feelings that come out of the decision to follow what is good. "How can anything that feels so good be wrong?" our natural reasoning goes. This is a source of all kinds of addictions and immoralities in our world today.

But we hear these arguments at other levels as well, for example, in the government. If you are looking for examples of bad thinking and reasoning, the government is always a good place to look! In many situations being dealt with by the government, you will hear one side appealing to some standard and the other appealing to emotion. And both sides use this tactic depending on the topic being debated. For example, in the first half of 2011, the US got involved in supporting the war against Moamar Ghaddafi in Libya. In the summer, there was a debate. One side said, "The President violated the war powers act by getting us involved in Libya without consulting Congress," (the appeal to the standard). Representatives of the other side said, (in essence), "Yeah, but that Ghaddafi is a really bad guy and we need to stop him from killing all those people so it is okay for the President to do whatever he wants to accomplish that," (the appeal to emotions). I am not bringing up this particular situation to take sides or to suggest that the reader should take sides. In fact, very similar statements were made by opposite sides of the aisle when the US invaded Iraq. It is only to show how the standard versus emotion argument takes place at so many levels. Listen for it in the news and you will hear people from many walks of life justifying their position with emotional arguments, "It can't be wrong if it feels right."

I think we are just plain confused. In my understanding of the being formed in the image of God, I believe that we were given a desire for justice and also given a full range of emotions with which to experience life. One difference between us and God is that while God experiences emotion, God's emotions are never out of order. His standard of justice never changes and His emotions apparently follow according to the standard—they are reactions to the standard. In the Old Testament prophets, who I admit are a bit cumbersome to read, there is a pattern that goes something like this:

1. People have not met God's standard
2. Therefore, God is justifiably angry with them
3. And God's standard of justice demands action

Because people are confused about how emotion interacts with justice, they sometimes have trouble with an "angry God" that seems prevalent in the Old Testament (but who does show up in the New Testament also—Acts 5:1–11 as an example). They think that God is some sort of whimsical creature who flies off the handle and wipes people out in a temper tantrum kind of way. But those people are missing first, how serious and real God's standard is and second, how the emotions are a reaction to people's violation of the standard. The standard and the violation of it—not the emotion—are what are determining the action. Put another way, the emotions are simply a side effect of the adherence to the standard and the carrying out of justice, not the cause of it.

This works in positive ways, too. For those who understand it and apply it in the area of marriage, the intellectual commitment of a

1 Corinthians 13 kind of love is rewarded over time by a depth of emotional love that grows deeper over time; a love that is so much richer than the surface emotional love in which we "fall." It's a love that you can't fall out of because you never fell into it in the first place!

Even as I write this, I wonder about God's real plan for the love of marriage. I am moving in to the realm of speculation right now but it is reasonable to remember that for most of human history, including in many cultures today, marriage partnerships were not based on two people "falling in love" (emotion) the way we understand it today. Instead, they were at least on some level "arranged" if only by the limited access to available possible partners. Marriage was a commitment to continue a community or family line and I wonder if the gift of God to that commitment was that the bonds of marriage generated an emotional reward that followed the commitment? Falling in love is easy. Kids do it all the time just walking around the mall or going to summer camp. Unfortunately, many adults have not given up on the rush that comes with falling in love and are still seeking an emotional fix. Like junior and senior high school kids, they move from relationship to relationship. And with wonderful tools like those available on the internet, it's easier than ever!

Enough random speculating about marriage—after all, this is hardly a marriage book. But here is the bigger question, which impacts marriage and all human relationships: Are our emotions determining our thoughts and attitudes about right and wrong for ourselves and thereby for others? Knowing what we know even about our own emotions, much less those of others, is this the kind of thinking that will produce stable relationships in families, communities or in the world? Emotions are almost by definition unstable and unpredictable and definitely not a solid foundation on which to assess the rightness or wrongness of anyone's ideas, opinions or behaviors; not our own and not others. We are in the middle of a struggle between our hearts (emotions) and our minds (intellect) and in getting these two parts of our being out of order, we may be losing both!

The Should Do—
Do Do Gap

We have gotten confused regarding standards of what is right and what is wrong and we have this on-going collision inside our hearts and minds. More than that, we are confused because while we have standards of good and evil within us, we are not able to meet those standards in our own lives even as we use those same standards to judge the behavior of others! What in the world is going on here? Here is picture of what seems to be going on inside most people's heads.

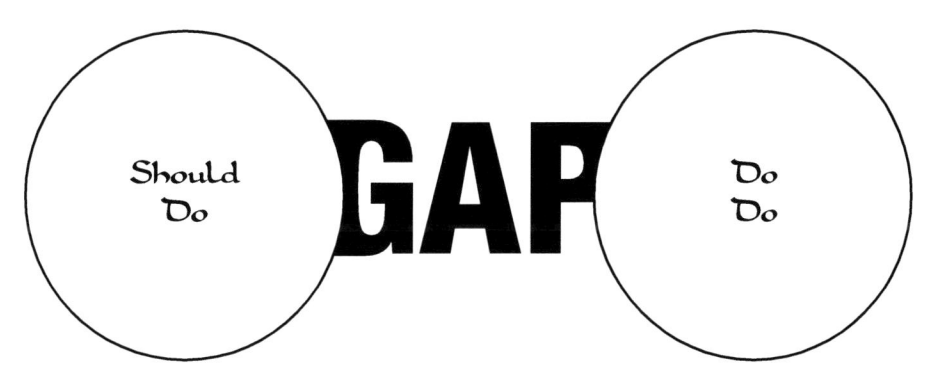

Should Do **GAP** **Do Do**

The Big Bite Theory says that being made in the image of God gives us this internal sense of justice—of what is good and evil. We know at a deep level that there are some things which are right and some which are wrong (the "Should Do") and we can't escape the quiet but persistent voice in our soul that some things just aren't right. And when those rights, as we understand them, are violated (by our own or others' "Do Do," and yes, this is an intentional pun), we believe that judgment is warranted. Even people who believe that we should be tolerant of everyone's opinions and ideas get really annoyed with people who dare to suggest that some ideas may be wrong. "How can you be so intolerant??!" they exclaim in an ironic condemnation of thinking which is different from theirs.

But forgetting the judgment of others, what about the gap that exists between our own "Should Do" and our "Do Do?" This is a very real problem for us and I believe a big part of the reason why we have gotten so confused that what *feels* good has become more important than what *is* good in determining our conscious standards. When there is a gap between what we Should Do and what we Do Do, our minds require us to do something about that gap. We basically have two choices.

The first choice is we can repent. We can admit that what we Do Do is wrong and we work to return our behavior (our Do Do) to the standard (the Should Do).

The second choice is to justify. We can use our brains to generate good intellectual reasons why our Do Do does not match our Should Do.

Our Do Do's are typically emotionally driven, especially when our Do Do's conflict with our Should Do's. So another way of looking at closing the gap between the two is to say that we have to drag one circle toward the other. In the first case, we admit that our emotions have led us to do something that conflicts with our understanding of what is right. We change our behavior and drag the Do Do circle on top of the Should Do circle trusting that the benefit of being true to our Should Do foundation will outweigh the sacrifice involved in not doing what we want to do. We choose to believe that what IS good will be better in the long run, than what FEELS good now.

In the second case, we drag the Should Do circle on top of the emotional Do Do circle and develop intellectual justifications to cover the emotionally driven Do Do circle, which has now become the foundation on which our understanding of good and evil rests. I believe that this is what our current American culture has moved toward. Intellectual truths based on absolutes of right and wrong are no longer considered to carry weight in the conversation and so we are left to develop our own ideas. Intellect is now used to justify emotional passions.

When we make emotional "feel goods" the foundation, the goal in our lives becomes being happy. When we are happy, things are good and when we are not, something needs to change so that we can be happy again. Not only that, but as we believe that people are basically good and therefore should feel good, it also becomes our goal to make sure that others are happy as well. But happiness is fleeting and we can't control the reactions of others. In its worst state, life becomes a series of frustrations and disappointments in ourselves and in others punctuated by brief periods of "happiness" when we think that things are finally the way they should be. Those familiar with addiction will recognize the cycle in which many addicts and enablers live.

In many ways, our culture has become addicted to emotional happiness. Of course, the problem with addiction is that after a time, the "fix" only serves to maintain the situation. It no longer thrills like it did so there is a desire for either more frequent or more intense experiences. One way that I see this played out in our current culture is on the television, where it is an emotional roller coaster. Even the so-called news channels are slickly produced exposés of the most recent insanity that used to be reserved for *The National Enquirer* and like tabloids. If there are debates about real issues, they are often emotional shouting matches well-choreographed by "mediators" priming the pump of conflict and emotionalism that make the experience one sure to thrill.

In the end, when the Do Do circle becomes our foundation, the goal is emotional in nature and we know or experience truth based on what our emotions tell us. Thinking that people are good at their core is a part of this cycle in that it focuses more on what we emotionally want to believe about people than what the evidence points to in terms of the actual behavior of generations of people in general and people we know specifically, including and perhaps especially ourselves.

Here is a summary of the circles and what they represent in the picture I am trying to paint:

○ Should Do   ○ Do Do

Source	God given conscience	Pride, self-serving desires
Decisions based on	Intellect—What IS right	Emotion—What FEELS right
Goal	Contentment	Happiness
Process	Emotions follow/submit to intellect	Intellect used to justify emotions

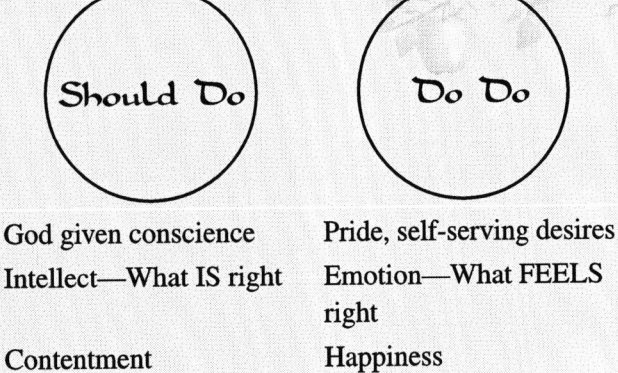

When we make our Do Do conform with our Should Do, we end up with more behaviors and actions, which make sense to our value system and lead to more stable emotions that ultimately bring us greater long term contentment and even happiness. However, if we allow ourselves to indulge in modifying our Should Do to conform with our Do Do, the result can be increasing chaos and a self-centered, self-gratification focused life that is ultimately insecure and unstable.

Can you see the gap in your own life? What do you do when you find yourself in that gap? Can you see the evidence of how our culture, or perhaps any human culture, deals with the gap? Is our American culture looking more Should Do focused or are we looking more like we are wallowing in our Do Do?

Painting with a broad brush here, but the assumption of fool's good thinking is that the nature of people is good and since being happy is what makes us feel good we should therefore expect to be happy because that is good and we are good. Following this thinking, bad things in our lives become exceptions to the rule of goodness and require an explanation. Depending on the kind of bad things that happen to us as people, we come up with varying explanations. If the situation is a fairly minor one we might default to blaming another person ("Who put this dent in my car?") or assign the problem to having one of those mystical bad days ("That's the third time I have stubbed my toe today!").

However, if the bad thing that happens is more significant or we begin to perceive a pattern of bad things happening in our lives, we start looking for bigger explanations. We might appeal to life not being fair ("Why do bad things always happen to me?") or appeal to some higher purpose for our lives that is negative ("I am just one of those people who attracts bad things. I'm a bad luck charm."). I have known a lot of kids and not a few adults who have walked down this path.

Eventually with significant experiences, thoughts turn to God. With the worldview that promotes the innate goodness of people comes the expectation that good things and happiness are the expected and maybe even deserved norm. Life is supposed to be good. Therefore, when the bad things come, one explanation is that God is hard. People with this mindset will almost inevitably ask some version of this common question, "If God is supposed to be good, why does he let all these bad things happen?" I want to be clear in saying that I believe that this is a legitimate question that needs to be pursued by anyone who is seeking to understand God. But the question doesn't make sense unless one is living on a foundation where good things are expected as the norm and bad things as the exception.

The worldview that comes out of the Big Bite Theory brings with it a truth that bad things are the natural consequence of our universal human tendency to be self-centered and to believe that we know what is right and what is wrong. We should expect bad things to happen. Life is hard. God becomes a source of comfort and hope in bad situations because while life is hard, God is good. In the fullest application of this foundation, I suppose the correct question would not be "Why does God allow bad things?" but instead, "Why do I not experience more bad things in my life?" The point is that the formation of the question starts with understanding one's underlying assumptions about what is normal and expected.

Sometimes church folk have more trouble with this than people who do not have an active faith. Church folk have believed that God is good but may have also bought the idea that life is good. When one of their children is diagnosed with a life threatening disease or their spouse has a heart attack and dies suddenly, or they experience some other tragedy, they are forced to confront their goodness doctrine head on. God is good and life is good. But now this bad thing has happened. One of these two assumptions is wrong. But many people don't even realize that they have the life is good assumption as a part of their thinking so they begin to question God's goodness. "I must have been wrong about God." It never occurs to many to say, "I must have been wrong about life."

Did Things Really Change?
The Collision of Faith and Science, Creation and Evolution

Let's go back 250 years or so. At that time, there was a movement in the American colonies to rebel against the rule of England due to the unjust treatment by that government of the residents of the colonies. We won't do a history lesson, but focus on one aspect of what the leaders of the colonies believed. They believed that 1) the King and the English government were unjust and morally corrupt, and 2) that ANY government that invested power in one or a small group of people would become unjust and morally corrupt. There are lots of arguments by scholars who actually know something about this regarding the faith beliefs of the founding fathers. But in general, they had a Genesis view of the nature of man. They believed that people were inherently broken. They believed that government was necessary for enforcing order but that it could not be trusted because it was made up of people. Our whole system of representative government and the checks and balances in the federal branches, eventually replicated in almost all of the states (Nebraska has only one Congressional body), came about as a result of this worldview. Read what Thomas Paine had to say at the time:

> *"Society is produced by our wants, and government by wickedness; the former promotes our happiness* positively *by uniting our affections, the latter* negatively *by restraining our vices."*

> *"For were the impulses of conscience clear, uniform, and irresistibly obeyed, man would need no other lawgiver; but that not being the case, he finds it necessary to surrender up a part of his property to furnish means for the protection of the rest; and this*

he is induced to do by the same prudence which in every other case advises him out of two evils to choose the least." (Common Sense—1776)

As best as I can understand it, Thomas Paine had great faith in the ability of people to regulate themselves into a society that would require little government oversight, and spoke out mostly against the evils of the monarchy as a means of authority in the colonies or indeed, anywhere! But in speaking about government, even he recognized that without some authority, people's unrestrained "vices" would corrupt the society. He also recognized that an unrestrained government would likewise be compromised by human vices. This was common thinking among the leaders of the United States at that time. It does not seem to be so now.

In some ways, the change in worldview regarding the nature of people can be seen to coincide with the advance of the theory of evolution specifically and science in general as being the best, and in some cases only acceptable way to view the world.

Prior to 200 years ago or so, most science was pursued in the interest of explaining the world that God created. It was assumed that the world, including people, came from God and an accurate understanding of any part of the world had to understand the world in the context of the larger God who was the source of the world.

The increase of science as the explanation of all things and the source of what is true has led to the opposite. It is assumed that the world came about through natural, scientifically explainable processes and that God must be understood in the context of the larger scientific world. In the old days, God created the world and people. In the new mindset, people have created God as an explanation for the unknowns in their experience. In the new view, it is expected that faith in God will become unnecessary as science slowly but surely explains all things. In the extreme of the new view, current faith in God is actually a dangerous thing and is responsible for much of the wrong that exists in the world. This view is promoted in such books as *God Is Not Great: How Religion Poisons Everything* by Christopher Hitchens and *The End of Faith* by Sam Harris.

In the current view, science/evolution as a worldview is moving to marginalize and eventually eliminate what that view sees as worthless superstition. The leading edge of this movement is advocating the ending of religious belief. It hasn't reached that point in most public discourse at the present time, but is certainly moving in that direction. One place to see that is in the public schools. In the very distant past, children were taught to read at least in part through use of the bible. In today's world, some schools I work in have eliminated the celebration of any holidays whatsoever. No Christmas parties. No Easter parties. No Halloween parties. All holidays are seen as treading into the area of personal belief and therefore not to be promoted or encouraged through any public institution. Even conversations about God are considered inappropriate in many classrooms, at least when it involves personal belief. There are schools that still teach some kind of religious history. I don't find that most schools in which I work are hostile to people of faith, but more dismissive. The message seems to be, "It is okay to believe whatever you want, but here at school we only talk about things that are true."

The language choice is intentional. Faith is considered outside the realm of truth in the scientific worldview. This is again found articulated openly at the leading edge of this worldview movement. Most people have not embraced this wholly, but their worldview is being built on a foundation that ultimately leads to the conclusion that faith is not true since it is not scientific. There really is a collision between faith and science. There is a competition for defining the big questions of life: How did we get here? Why do we exist? What happens after we die? These are traditionally questions that have been the exclusive domain of religion and philosophy. Science as a philosophy, like any good business, is trying to increase its market share and is offering people a choice of answers to those questions that lie outside the borders of traditional religion.

In my view, by entering into the world of big questions, science has in fact become a religion with its own doctrines, rituals, priests and pastors, and even denominations. One of the first ways I noticed that science knew it was becoming a religious option was from the back of cars.

I mentioned the Jesus fish emblems that some people have on their cars at the beginning of the book. I also mentioned the very clever fish with little feet with the word Darwin in the middle. These started appearing after the original Jesus fish had been around for a while. The first time I saw one, I laughed out loud. The little feet were an especially nice touch! But as I thought about it, it occurred to me that the people who promoted the use of the Jesus fish had originally done so to promote public testimony of their faith in Jesus. Faith in Jesus represents a certain worldview but is not necessarily contrary to believing that science has value or is useful for discovering truth. In fact, as mentioned, almost all science prior to 1800 was "faith based," and much of it since then as well. Read the writings of old time scientists like Newton and Pascal and you'll see faith (hint: It won't be mentioned in your high school science text!). Regarding the Jesus fish, I would venture to guess that the people who first produced those were not thinking of Jesus in relation to science at all.

But the people who came up with the Darwin fish were clearly going after those who believe in Jesus. In developing a mocking version of the Jesus fish, they were in effect saying that belief in Jesus is contrary to belief in Darwin and science in general. They were entering into a theological discussion that they themselves initiated, at least in this particular way. I'm okay with that. What makes the discussion difficult is when people from the scientific camp will not acknowledge that they are actively involved in a theological perspective. Issues related to faith come up and the radical scientific evolutionists will say in effect, "We're above that sort of thing. We believe in science."

I agree that the scientific worldview folks believe in science. They believe that science has the answers to the big questions of life in much the same way that I believe that my faith in the God of the bible expressed in the person of Jesus answers the big questions of life. There are some things that evolutionists accept on faith. Even though there isn't scientific proof of many aspects of evolution or origins of the universe or other related things, they have "faith" that one day these things will be known—through science.

In a similar way, although I have faith in God, I acknowledge that there are some questions that my faith simply cannot answer at this time. I don't know how God did or does everything he did or does. Similarly, I also believe that one day those things will be known—either when I die or at the return of Jesus. The main point is that both worldviews deal with unanswerable questions and believe that their worldview holds hidden answers that will one day be known. That is what faith is all about!

One main difference between the two is that while many who espouse scientific theology are passionate that their worldview necessarily ultimately excludes the possibility of an active God in the explanation of answers to the big questions, faith in God assumes that science can provide truthful explanations of the mysteries of what God has created. The first excludes the other. The second embraces the other.

Some are going to bothered by this whole argument since I am casting it in black and white and there are still many people in the middle who say they believe in both. My point is to look at the leading edge of the scientific theology mind set and look for evidence that the cultural norm is moving in that direction. One way to see this is to listen to media. Anytime scientific issues are touched on, it is clear that evolution is assumed as fact and any religious theology is never mentioned. I'm not a conspiracy kind of guy. I don't think there are media people getting together and saying, "Let's never mention God!" Instead, I believe it is the natural evidence of the shift in worldview that has taken place in our American culture. What was once a "theory" is now spoken of as assumed "fact." Listen for it on the radio or television and even in conversations with people in the world. I had one with a couple of college professors at a camp I was at. One was a paleontologist and I was commenting that sometimes people get paleontologists and archaeologists confused. My wife is an archaeologist and is often reminding people that she does not look for dinosaur bones. The wife of the paleontologist agreed and immediately commented somewhat sarcastically that "there are still some people who believe that dinosaurs and people walked on the earth together. There are lots of those in our state." This nice lady had no idea what I believed about anything as we had just happened to sit together in the cafeteria. But it was fairly clear from her tone that she believed that her perspective was fact and anything else was nonsense. And her freedom in sharing her perspective so quickly with someone she had just met showed an attitude that she believed that her perspective was the norm of the culture.

By now you might have guessed that I am not a scientist. I like science and am fascinated by the discoveries that are made almost daily in this technologically advanced time that we live in—compared to past generations that is! I am not a science-phoebe. I'm not afraid of science and do not believe that science is in any way a threat to my faith in God. I know that I am simply not knowledgeable or wise enough to ever be able to discern for sure how God brought things into being other than to believe that in ways far beyond my understanding, God made what "is" out of nothing. That being said, the science vs. faith conversation is a stumbling block issue for some people on both sides of the fence. For them, I heartily encourage reading Francis Collin's book *The Language of God*.

Unlike me, Dr. Collins actually knows something about science, having been the head of the Human Genome Project. "The Human Genome Project (HGP) is an international scientific research project with a primary goal of determining the sequence of chemical base pairs which make up DNA, and of identifying and mapping the approximately 20,000–25,000 genes of the human genome from both a physical and functional standpoint." (http://en.wikipedia.org/wiki/Human_Genome_Project) It was a massive project that took place between 1990 and 2003, with the project actually being completed two years ahead of schedule.

In *The Language of God*, Dr. Collins explains his understanding of the evolutionary process as science has discovered it thus far AND his own conclusion that there is something in the created nature of human beings that reflects that hand of a Creator God. He references the thoughts of C.S. Lewis who wrote about the moral law that we all are aware of but all of us violate at some level. And he references our need for a solution to our brokenness in the form of a savior who can rescue us from ourselves. Dr. Collin's book is a fine example of seeing both sides of the conversation and finding truth in both.

The whole worldview argument boils down to there needing to be an explanation for morality that fits the evidence and experience of people. If there is a moral standard, it has to come from somewhere. In the Genesis understanding, there is a source of morality outside of the human mind to which we are all held accountable. This standard is God and God's character, which is seen as both perfect and unchanging. People have been created in the image of God, and as such, they have an inner moral compass that points toward God. However, in the process of people coming up with our own definitions of good an evil (The Big Bite), we have lost our moorings, so to speak. So there is an internal struggle in each person's soul between what we were created to be and what we have become.

All of this requires the existence of an external standard—an absolute to which all people are held accountable. If that standard does not exist, then the whole question of morality and good and evil becomes meaningless. Without the external standard, the opinions of each individual person become just as "right" as the opinions of any other. And one of the common cries of our current American culture becomes true, "You can't tell me what to think. I can decide for myself what is right and wrong for me."

The problem with evolution and science devoid of God is that it eliminates the external standard from the conversation about morality. Without the external standard, there really is no ultimate good and evil and every moral decision becomes valid as long as the person making it really believes it. In some ways, the standard of belief in our culture today is how sincerely you believe what you believe, not whether what you believe actually makes any sense at all! And it seems to me that strict, so-called godless evolutionists are okay with that. As I understand the basic idea, survival is the ultimate good and reproducing what is more likely to survive is the ultimate goal. There isn't really a moral component to that. People are just like other living creatures that have come about on the earth with no more inherent value than any other.

To me this has some potential moral consequences that are difficult to accept. In the animal kingdom, eliminating the weak members of the herd is seen as beneficial. If the weak members of the herd are killed, then the members of the herd that reproduce will be stronger, resulting in a stronger future herd. But if human beings are just another kind of "herd"—you can see where this could lead. Frankly, it leads to Hitler and people like him who believe that elimination of a certain group of people is what is best for the overall "herd." A person with no external reference point and who accepts a purely godless, scientific explanation of our existence might fault the Hitlers of the world with identifying the wrong people as being the weak members of the herd. But on what grounds will that same person condemn the philosophy that says that weak herd members should be eliminated in the first place? In the purely scientific worldview, human beings are simply one branch of many in the evolution of life on the planet and that in the ultimate reality, a human life has no more value than a broccoli plant or a fly or one of those fish in the deep sea with a light hanging out the top of its head. Presumably, that angler fish with the light on its head exists because it represents the best of the best that branch of the evolutionary tree has to offer and almost by definition, weaker representatives have been eliminated through the years. In this thinking, what's "good" for the fish with the lights on their heads must also be good for people.

Some people reading this will likely think that I am being too simplistic; that the conversation is much more complex than this. But I am trying to look beyond the intellectual justifications to the underlying foundation on which the arguments are built. To get to an understanding of good and evil, good and evil have to be defined. If there is no comparative standard, then there really cannot be any good and evil, at least not in the ultimate sense. The foundation of the Genesis story is that people are uniquely created in the world in the image of God. That created image includes a longing for justice that conforms to God's character. Having been created in the image of God, we are also capable of thought and choice in a way not available to the other animals, or plants for that matter. In our ability to think, we have outthought God and decided we could make up our own minds about what is good and what is evil and there has been nothing but trouble ever since.

In the evolutionary foundation, people are one branch of an amoral process in which there is no real good and evil except for survival and reproduction and in which humanity has no unique value compared to anything else that is alive in the world. Discussions about good and evil may be useful in organizing society in a way that allows the gene pool to continue to flourish. However, moral opinions have no ultimate correctness. Survival and reproduction ARE the ultimate good.

Here is an interesting consequence of this avenue of belief. The basic understanding of undirected (godless) evolution is that species are continually improving. As natural selection takes place, strengths and improvements are selected and maintained in the gene pool while weaknesses and deficiencies are eliminated. The acceptance of this as the foundation for our existence has contributed strongly to the idea that people are basically good. After all, we are here aren't we? If we have made it to this point and we exist in this form, we must be good. And if we could look into the future a few thousand years, we can expect that people will be even better! Most people are not aware at the conscious level that this acceptance of the purely scientific explanation for our existence is influencing their understanding of the nature of people. But it leads to defining people as being good.

Meanwhile, we continue to kill each other fighting over territory and profits and ideals. We use what the planet yields with little concern regarding what future generations will have to deal with or clean up. We accumulate resources as a definition of success while millions around the world go hungry and thirsty. We have regular road rage at idiots who cut us off in traffic, judging them as morally inferior as we curse at them and wave fingers in their direction. We lie on our taxes and sneak peeks at pornographic websites. We cheat on our wives and husbands and neglect and abuse our kids. We worry and are afraid that we are being taken advantage of in some way. We hold up Mother Theresa and Gandhi and Jesus and disaster relief efforts as examples of human goodness in action, when it is probably more accurate to hold them up as exceptions to the rule of selfishness and exploitation in which the majority engage.

I don't believe that in my lifetime there will be resolution to the evolution/creation debate. I do think that sometimes both sides miss the bigger point and are arguing about the wrong thing. Creationists emphasize that God created everything and evolution is "wrong." They seem to think that if they can scientifically convince those who believe in evolution that they are wrong, that those same people will then turn to God. But the issue is deeper than the science laid on top of it. Are good and evil real constructs or just the meaningless labels developed by an organized society that evolved in an essentially random manner?

The devotees of the evolution "religion" trivialize the beliefs of those who believe in a living, active God and in an ironic twist, they claim a moral high ground in that they do not have to lean on the God crutch for their understanding of life. They are able to blame the brokenness of the world on religious belief, a relatively easy argument to make actually! But if the real issue is not the religious belief of people but people in general, it's a whole different argument that evolution cannot easily explain. For example, Stalin's Russia was not a religious problem but a power problem.

The problem with arguments about the scientific proof of evolution is that both sides think the people on the other side are stupid (remember the paleontologist's wife in the cafeteria?). Assuming stupidity is hardly a good foundation on which to start a conversation about the meaning of life! During the 2008 presidential campaign season, there was quite a bit of conversation in my family, and I'm sure many others, when Sarah Palin was selected by John McCain to be the Republican vice-presidential candidate. I have several members of my extended family who are interested in politics and are willing to comment about it via family e-mails. They come from both ends of the political spectrum, which was particularly interesting during this campaign. Those who are more from the left side were aghast at this nomination. One e-mail in particular was memorable to me. It said, "I could never vote for someone who believes in creationism." There was no development of the reasons—just a clear assumption that anyone who believes in creationism must be lacking in intelligence and therefore not equipped to be in leadership, apparently at any level.

This kind of "litmus test" thinking takes place in many areas in our culture (think abortion, for example) and to me is just one more bit of evidence of the deeper issue at work here. As people, we believe that our opinions are correct and that anyone who disagrees with our opinions is clearly lacking in either brains or ethics. At the same time, we are not supposed to be judgmental and we know that on some level. In the religious mind, it has to do with God being the judge. In the non-religious mind, it has to do with the cultural value of tolerance. An interesting dynamic emerges involving internal judgments based on our knowledge of good and evil. We then find others who "judge" the same way we do, for example in churches, political parties, service organizations, intellectual groups, or just our friends. Then in our groups of like judges, we like to say that our group is not judgmental! Ask yourself if the groups with which you associate most frequently or to which you choose to belong would describe themselves as judgmental.

We judge all the time! It's not just that we judge those who are not like us in thought or deed or whatever. We are also judging those who are like us. We judge them as meeting our picture of a person with whom we want to be associated. This is just as much based on our inner knowledge of good and evil as are our judgments of those we don't want to associate with. It's all judgment, all the time. It's all we know! For certain, many people are able to overcome this natural tendency and choose to associate with people who are different from themselves on purpose. Initially, this takes place across easily defined boundaries such as language, ethnicity, race, etc. At this level, overcoming differences is challenging but doable and rewarding. It gets more difficult as a person chooses to associate in relationships of mutual respect with people who hold opinions which are diametrically opposed to their own.

Regardless of the level of difference, we recognize that in choosing to associate with people who are different, we have to overcome our natural tendency not to do so. While most people will acknowledge that this is true, there tends to be little discussion about the implications of this natural tendency in terms of the broader "nature of people." If our natural tendency is to collect in groups with like opinions and characteristics and to think less of those who are different, then our natural tendency can also be said to be that we tend to judge with the result of exclusion of others. I can't see that as being a naturally "good" thing. So, ARE people good at their core or have we allowed ourselves to only see what's on the surface, the fool's gold of cultural morality, and assume that deeper inside is more good stuff?

Good God/Bad God

Everyone is going to serve some kind of god. Bob Dylan was right about that! We serve whatever or whomever we put in the place of a higher power even if that higher power is simply our own opinions. For some, the higher power is the God of the bible. For others it is the truth of science. And there are many other options. We have constructs in our minds about what are the higher truths to which we hold ourselves (and often unwilling others!) accountable.

When we accept the often unspoken but culturally prevalent belief that people are good inside, there is an even deeper and less spoken assumption that follows: If people are basically good, and we are people, then if we seek after the good that is within us, then we must be seeking after real good. This becomes a theological issue for those who believe in a higher power. But even for those who do not accept the existence of a higher power, what you think about the nature of people has a profound impact on what you believe are the higher truths by which you will make choices you define as good or evil. For now, this discussion will be in the area of defining the god that we will serve.

We define our god based on what we think is right and wrong, good and evil. If a person understands the human tendency to determine good and evil on his or her own, and through that tendency to screw things up quite a bit, that person will be more inclined to seek outside information about what god might be like. But even committed believers in God who do not understand this most basic part of our character and who accept the cultural understanding of the nature of people are going to have a tendency to "trust in their own understanding" as it says in Proverbs 3. But as we have talked about, we kind of get confused with thinking that what feels good, is good. And if we think that what feels good to us is what is going to please the good god that we serve, we are often sadly mistaken.

The best example of this that I can share with you involves a young man who attends our church. Dennis began experiencing seizures at an early age and he has struggled with special needs his whole life. Dennis has difficulty with reading and indeed all academic skills. He was in special education throughout his school years and has moved in and out of a number of supported employment situations, often losing positions due to his "anger issues." Dennis is in his late 20s and continues to live with his parents. I use Dennis as an example because in his "specialness" he has done in a way that is easy to see what many of us do in more subtle ways.

Dennis has a great sense of rhythm and a pretty good singing voice. He is amazing at video games. He is very verbal and in many ways quite perceptive about many things. Dennis loves movies, especially fantasy and super hero movies. In his love for entertainment media, he has developed a desire to be a famous actor and/or singer. He routinely talks about moving to California so that he can follow his dreams that almost always involve the current teenage female star, who he is going to meet and probably marry.

I have known Dennis for about 10 years and have talked with him a number of times about fantasy and reality. But Dennis believes that his "goals" and his "dreams" are the only things that are going to make him happy. "I just want to be famous so that I can be important." Fame in the entertainment industry has become Dennis's god. He goes to church and believes in Jesus and sings about Jesus with the church worship team. But the god that he serves is Fame in the entertainment industry.

It's hard not to feel bad for Dennis. He has a lot of limitations that have caused him and his family many difficulties through the years. And he has dreams and goals that are not realistic and will never be fulfilled. This is hard to write even in this context because we live in a world where we teach that "you can do anything if you work hard enough and believe in yourself." "If you dream it, you can achieve it!" I am not supposed to say to Dennis that he will never be famous. I am not supposed to say that his dreams are fantasies and can't be realized. "I have always wanted to be Spiderman," I tell Dennis (this is actually true!), "But I never will be." He agrees with me because he knows that Peter Parker is not a real person. "But famous people are real," Dennis says, "so I could be famous." I want to tell Dennis that famous people aren't really "real"; they are more like the cardboard cutouts you see at the movie theater than real people. But I know that it is difficult for any of us to understand when reality and dreams collide.

The dynamic so obviously at work in Dennis is common. People in our world today believe that emotions are valid sources of information. Things that make us feel good (or we think would make us feel good), become goals regardless of whether those goals are in keeping with our given gifts, talents, abilities, or even what is best for us. We then serve our goals, which become something like gods to us. But these gods can never satisfy. They cannot bring us the happiness we crave or the contentment we need. So Dennis and I and so many others seek after a god that tells us that we are never good enough. Since we have decided that serving this god is what is best for us, when we are not able to meet that god's expectations and therefore are not "happy," we have to find an explanation. I find that the explanations people develop take two directions. Both are destructive.

The first explanation is that I am a failure and the second is that God is against me or is punishing me. Meanwhile, the real God of the bible is saying all along, "Dennis, you are acceptable and valuable exactly as you are. You don't need to do anything more to be worthy and important." But with our distorted definitions of good and evil we have so much trouble accepting this God given affirmation of our value.

In the Old Testament in the book of Isaiah, this concept is laid out in this passage:

"Half of the wood he burns in the fire. Over it, he prepares his meal; he roasts his meat and eats his fill. He also warms himself and says, 'Ah, I am warm; I see a fire.' From the rest of the

wood he makes a god, his idol; he bows down to it and worships. He prays to it and says, 'Save me; you are my god.' They know nothing, they understand nothing; their eyes are plastered over so they cannot see, and their minds closed so they cannot understand. No one stops to think, no one has the knowledge of understanding to say, 'Half of it I used for fuel; I even baked bread over its coals, I roasted meat and ate. Shall I make a detestable thing from what is left? Shall I bow down to a block of wood?' He feeds on ashes, a deluded heart misleads him; he cannot save himself or say, 'Is not this thing in my right hand a lie?'"
—Isaiah 44:16–20

In looking at this passage, one way to consider it is in terms of economics. For most of us in our culture, a block of wood does not have much economic value. In that time, wood was a commodity. It represented not only something with a variety of uses, but it also was an economic resource necessary for supporting oneself. These resources were the currency of the day. One needed wood to eat and keep warm and so on. In this way, "You take this resource necessary to provide for yourself and you take part of it and make it your god."

Certainly it is not difficult for us to see how we have abstracted material goods like wood to a representational system where we don't deal directly with materials but now deal with money. And from there, it is even easier to see how money has become the god of our age. The bible does not say that money is evil, only that "the love of money is a root of all kinds of evil" (1 Timothy 6:10), and that money is in competition for the position of "god" in our lives (Matthew 6:24). Today we take part of the money to feed, clothe and house ourselves, and the rest we use to fashion ourselves a god, a god who can never satisfy because the god we have made can neither hear nor act.

A second way to look at the Isaiah passage in today's terms is to look at the commodities that are valued in today's economy. While physical resources are always required, we live an economy that is increasingly based on intellectual capital. The mind has become the most valuable resource in our culture. With this in mind, we can take the Isaiah passage and translate it into today's terms: "You take half of your mind and use it to make a living, and the other half and use it to make up for yourself a god that makes sense to you." A god that makes sense to us is one based on what we think is good. But our limited vision means we get a god who has to be understood by our minds not a God whose mind contains the entire universe. We get a god that we define and so must be contained within the limits of our understanding, not a God who defines us and sees what we cannot.

As with my friend Dennis, many people want to have both gods. They set up goals and dreams of their own making and understanding and serve them first and foremost. But many also want to hold onto a vague idea of "somebody upstairs." And as in the case of Dennis, they often draw the conclusion: "I feel like God isn't there. I feel like he isn't helping me." If God isn't helping me do what I want to do, then maybe he isn't there at all. When in reality, Dennis is a great guy right now with many things that he could be doing to be productive and in doing those things, he could get much closer to the satisfaction for which he and all of us are looking. Instead, he continues to believe that his satisfaction must come through the goals that he has defined as good; through satisfying the god of Fame he has created.

If we require a god to only do things that are completely explainable by our own minds, then we become greater than God—our understanding is over God. If we begin to look for a god that is greater than our understanding and who is not accountable to our expectations and desires, then we are put in a position of having to question everything that we believe about right and wrong and good and evil. One leads to confusion and frustration. The other can lead to contentment even in difficult circumstances.

At a recent meeting of the community group addressing poverty (of which I am a member), we had a discussion about the importance of spirituality. The discussion was started by giving everyone a page with printed traffic signs and then people were asked to pick the sign that best represented their spirituality. After a lot of sharing, we were asked to draw a picture the showed what spirituality meant to us. Here is a recreation of what I drew.

The person (me) is standing at a fork in the road. I went with the traffic sign motif to show that I was paying attention! One fork leads to a BIG God who encompasses and defines me but who is bigger than me and in fact leads to me having a much smaller view of my own self-importance. The other path leads to me with a BIG HEAD that encompasses and defines God. However, I am now standing on nothing and have no protection around me. I have taken the left road far too often in my life.

So the nice looking atheist on the billboard I drove past says, "I can be good without God." Yup. That's actually true as long as you get to define good yourself and don't mind if I define it differently. Furthermore, the guys who shoot abortion doctors and the suicide bombers and pedophiles get their own definitions of good as well. Even the standard, "You can do anything you want as long as you don't hurt anyone else," has to come from somewhere outside of people's minds if it is to have any validity at all. Otherwise, the crazy people who do real harm but think they are doing good are just as "good" as anyone else. This is "fool's good."

Fool's Gold Is Hard—Real Gold Is Moldable

Fool's gold is good for what it is good for pretty much as soon as you find it in the ground. It's shiny and pretty and you can pick it up and separate it from its environment fairly easily. But it is also hard and brittle and you can't do much with it. Real gold is a bit more complex. It is embedded in lots of other not so valuable stuff and must be refined and purified to get that junk out. But, once refined and purified, it is also flexible and can be formed into all kinds of shapes and forms.

Using these as images for what is inside of us leads to an understanding of why it is hard for us to change and grow. If a person is living according to his or her own beliefs about what is good and evil and is not regularly testing those beliefs against an outside reference point, it is hard to see the need to change. In fact, the whole idea that I may need to change becomes somewhat offensive, as has become the case in our society today. I hear it a lot from kids in the schools where I work. In various situations and to various people I hear kids say some version of "You can't tell me what to think." Now on some level, there is a truth in that which is valuable in terms of being able to use one's own mind to make one's own decisions and stand up for one's beliefs and so on. We teach this at an early age with the proverbial, "If your friends jumped off a bridge, would you jump, too?" However, I rarely hear, "You can't tell me what to think," in the context of resisting negative peer pressure. Rather, kids, including old kids (translate: adults), are referencing a foundational belief that each person can make up his or her own mind and thus determine truth for themselves.

Some might argue that thinking this way would make a person open to learning new things about what is true and good in the world. In what may seem somewhat counterintuitive, I find that this way of thinking often produces resistance to growth. People do not feel the need to grow because their minds already contain what is true, *for them.* They don't need to know anything else about truth because they already know what they know. Their minds contain what is true for them. This is not to say that a person of this foundation is not open to learning. Many people love to learn and be exposed to new things. But when the foundation is, "What I think is right is right and outside information can only impact me if I allow it to," a person is going to have more difficulty experiencing personal change, sometimes in needed areas.

On the other hand is the person who starts with a foundation based on the Genesis idea that as humans we have developed a personal sense of good and evil that is inclined to be at best a distortion of what is really true and at worst a complete perversion. This person recognizes that personal motivations and pride color every thought and judgment they have. A person who has accepted this foundation as being an accurate reflection of their own inner thinking starts new learning from a point of view that says, "Everything that I believe about everything must be suspect, because it is tainted by my tendency to judge right and wrong on my own terms." This person is more likely to be able to use new information and insight to effect real change in their lives.

One might think that the second kind of thinking would be more prevalent in a church setting where the Genesis concepts are talked about some of the time anyway! But one of the main problems with the whole "knowledge of good and evil" problem is that it operates below the level of our consciousness. I am messing with the church world now, but I have encountered many in that world who would agree that the Genesis account is informative but who also believe that people are basically good and who operate from a perspective that their opinions actually matter in terms of what is right and wrong. And for many of those people, change is extremely difficult.

There are many people who go to church every week although not as many as there once were! Many people go through all the motions of religion. They dress a little nicer on Sunday morning. They volunteer as greeters or ushers or servers or whatever. They stand up at the right times and sit down at the right times. They know all the prayers and sing when they are supposed to. And then when the teaching starts, usually in the form of a sermon, they either fall asleep, sometimes literally, or they nod in agreement. "Amen, pastor!" "That's good stuff, pastor." "I agree with that!" And so on. The attitude of both groups is, "I already know this stuff." Then they leave the church building after the appropriate fellowship time following service and *nothing changes in their hearts or minds or actions*. Nothing changes because at the foundation, many and maybe most people don't believe that they really need to change. And the longer we stay the same, the harder it is to see the need to change. Our ability to justify our current state is a part of the problem.

In my life, I came to a better understanding of this when I began to ask myself this question when I read the bible: "Who do you think you are?" This is especially useful in reading the gospel accounts of the life of Jesus but can be used for anything in there. I am no different than most. I want to be the good guy in a story and believe that I am a good person. So when I began to follow Jesus in earnest, I would read about Jesus and his teachings and interactions with others and would almost always identify with Jesus. So if I had a mental picture of the situation, I was always standing right next to Jesus functioning primarily as chief cheerleader: "You go, Jesus!" "You tell 'em, Jesus." "You really showed 'em that time, Jesus." When I put myself in the story, I was always one of the good guys.

Everyone does this. You can see it with kids. There are some kids that get into lots of trouble. They are angry, disobedient, and mean. They are defiant when confronted and don't seem to care about the punishment. There may be many reasons why they are that way and there are usually sad stories associated with those reasons. Leaving that aside for the moment, these kids have turned out to be the "bad guys" in the stories of their lives at home, at school, and in the community. But if you can get one of those kids into a conversation about the latest superhero movie and have a sufficiently comfortable setting in which to ask the question and you ask the kid who he wants to be in the movie, the kid will identify with the hero. He wants to be the good guy. In the Genesis story, the image of God has been imprinted on every human heart and everyone wants to be the good guy because there is a part of every human that wants to be like the image in which he or she was made.

I will acknowledge freely that there are some kids and many adults who have simply reached the conclusion that they are not good and never can be. Either they have tried to be good and it didn't work out or they have received so many messages about their non-goodness that they have believed that it must be true. But in my experience working with kids, even these kids wish they could be the hero. They want to be the good guy.

Back to reading bible stories. If we understand that Jesus is the "image of the invisible God" as the bible says (Colossians 1:15), then we understand that God's desire to make each of us more like Jesus ("to be conformed to the likeness of his Son"—Romans 8:29) is a desire to make us more like himself; to bring us back into the image in which we were created. So we can logically conclude that we should be reading about Jesus with the understanding that we should be more like him in terms of attitude and behavior. Again, this is a point with which most people who attend Christian churches would agree. However, in order to be more like something, we must be able to see the gap between the thing we are to be more like and ourselves. And if we start from a perspective that basically believes that we are good already and if when we read about Jesus we see ourselves on his side then we are focusing on the sameness, how we are like Jesus, not on the difference between Jesus and ourselves. Real change becomes very difficult.

We can't see the need for the change because we identify with Jesus and think at a very deep level, "That's just what I would have done." This happens at such a deep level that we are not always even aware that we are doing it. But we do it all the time. Then the commutative property that we learned in early elementary math kicks in and we really get in trouble. The commutative property basically says that if two things are equal, they are equal even if you change the order. In this case, if Jesus does the same thing I would have done (if I am added to Jesus), then what I do is the same thing Jesus would do if he were in my place (Jesus is added to me). We begin to assume that since we agree with Jesus when we read the stories about him, it follows logically that he must agree with us when we form our opinions and beliefs. Both orders equal truth. Here's a visual representation:

$$a + b = c \quad\quad then \quad\quad b + a = c$$
$$Jesus + Me = truth \quad therefore \quad Me + Jesus = truth$$

People have been getting excited about causes that were important to them for many, many years and inviting Jesus to come along with them, almost as a mascot! It's a chicken/egg situation. Which came first—the truth of Jesus or my strong, emotional opinion? Do I have faith in a real God who determines what is right and wrong or do I cast God in my own image based on what I have decided is right and wrong? Am I accountable to God or is he accountable to me?

When I began to get this, I started asking the question, "Who do you think you are?" as a way to step back from my initial cheerleader role and instead to look at Jesus' interactions with people and ask myself with as much honesty as I could muster if I was more like Jesus in the story or more like the people to whom he was talking. When Jesus tells the arrogant rich young ruler, "One thing you still lack," am I more like Jesus or more like the rich young ruler? When Jesus says to Martha, "You are worried and upset about many things, but only one thing is needed," am I more like Jesus or more like Martha? When Jesus says to the Pharisees and teachers of the law, "You say, if we had lived during the time of our forefathers we would not have taken part with them in shedding the blood of the prophets," (Even the Pharisees and the teachers of the law wanted to be the good guys when they read the stories of the prophets!) am I more like Jesus or am I more like the Pharisees and teachers of the law?

Try it! You won't like it. It's uncomfortable to see yourself not as the hero but as being exposed by the hero. But quickly it develops into an easy way to see the gap between yourself and the image of the model of goodness. Quickly, the need for real change becomes evident and the natural tendency to rely on your own understanding painfully obvious. Quickly, your appreciation of the grace and mercy of Jesus will grow. And done correctly, you will begin to understand at a deeper level than ever before that you are important and loved beyond anything you could ever expect not because you are shiny with fool's gold goodness, but because you are precious with real gold value. You matter to God and he values you.

Sadly, I don't see this kind of approach to faith among most people who claim to follow Jesus or at least who attend Christian churches. When I say "sadly," it isn't because of the crazies who invoke the name of Jesus to kill people or protest at military personnel funerals or start their own bizarre cults. Those things are sad on their own merits, or lack of the same. No, I am sad for people who are cheating themselves of the opportunity to see the gap between themselves as they are and themselves as they could be through the refining grace and mercy of a God who loves them in spite of themselves. When a person has the foundational belief that people are basically good, he or she is put in the position of responding to bible teachings and church climate by proving to others and to themselves that "I am on the good side." When conflict arises, emotions tend to follow as at a deep level, beneath the level of consciousness in most cases, our fundamental assumptions about ourselves and the nature of people is being challenged. If two people are both following Jesus and have different opinions on a subject, then someone must be wrong. The idea that I could be wrong when I have "the knowledge of good and evil" within me causes defensive action and often defensive emotions. I have to either defend and prove my opinion or begin to look at deeper assumptions about who I am and who God is.

Now this gets a bit abstract but let me try to paint a picture that is in my head but that is hard to put into words. This whole thing is not about who is right and who is wrong in any given argument or on any given issue or decision. It's about why those who think they are right are right and the others are wrong and it applies to individuals on both sides of the argument.

Let's just say that there is a disagreement at church about whether the church should remove the pews and purchase more modern seating or keep the traditional and more formal pews. (This, by the way, is only a marginally hypothetical example in my experience!) And let's say further that God actually has an opinion about this issue; a dubious assumption in this case but these are the kinds of things we argue about in church! One side of the argument agrees with God and one side, by definition, does not. One side is right and one side is wrong.

But BOTH sides are wrong if they spend their time and energy trying to prove why God agrees with their side rather than seeking truly to discover what God really desires. More than that, they must be able to approach the process of discovery with a foundational understanding that "because of my tendency to develop strong opinions based on what I think is right rather than seeking God's truth, it is very possible that I am wrong about this situation." What is sad to see is that in these kinds of crazy disagreements that occur in church settings, this attitude is painfully rare on either side of the issue. And the deeper spiritual growth that is available to both sides is left wanting while seeds of division and bitterness are planted, watered, and in far too many cases, harvested.

When James, in his letter at the back part of the bible, tells us that we should use the word of God as a mirror (James 1:19–27), it is an old and easy application to remember that almost everyone who looks in a mirror fixes something. At the very least, people look in a mirror to make sure that nothing needs to be fixed. Hair's okay. No black specks in my teeth. No stains on my clothes from the lasagna at lunch. Even when things are okay, people adjust their hair or clothes or even just their posture when they look in a mirror. Those of us old enough to have watched the old Happy Days sitcom from the 70s laughed when Fonzie would look in the mirror and fix nothing but just say, "Hey!" and walk away. We laughed because we know that people don't do this as a rule.

But it seems to me that many people attending churches do this with the bible and bible teachings religiously every Sunday. I count myself among them. As we said before, we put on our Sunday best clothes, our Sunday best social skills, and our Sunday best smiles and nod in agreement with the Sunday sermon (when we are not nodding off!) and walk away with one of two reactions to what we have heard: 1) That was really good stuff. The pastor was right on today (I agree with everything the pastor said. I'm glad that I know that stuff.), or 2) Mr. So-and-So really needs to hear that message!

We love to hold mirrors in other people's faces. We are great at applying the need to change based on some inadequacy we identify in people who are not like us. Our tendency towards judgment is never more obvious than when we readily identify the faults of others. And we are good at it! We don't even need a sermon or a bible verse. We don't even have to be people of faith. We are naturally good at judging!

One more thing about the James passage. Although it seems clear that James is referring to the word of God as in the bible, it is also true that Jesus is the living Word of God. Another way to look at this passage is to see James as saying that we should not merely listen to and watch Jesus, but that we should allow the listening and watching of Jesus to expose us and through that exposure to mold and change us. Jesus came to fulfill the law (the word of God) not to abolish it (Matthew 5:17). He is the fulfillment of what God intended for us to be when we are in perfect relationship with him. He is our model and our perfect mirror. When we "look into" Jesus, we can focus on the ways that we are like him, or we can see how we are not like him. The first can build us up but can also harden us and make us resistant to needed change. We might be shiny on the outside ("I give 10% of all I earn to the work of God."), but unrefined on the inside ("This church depends on me. If it wasn't for my giving so much, we would have gone under years ago."). This is the fool's good principal in action.

Meanwhile, the world is out there having arguments about all kinds of things. But with the prevalent worldview increasingly that there are no absolute answers about right and wrong on any given issues, people in the world are ironically open to change in opinion in ways that many followers of Jesus are not! Without the concept of an absolute reference point, people who are both in the world and of the world accept that their opinion is only one of many and that there are many ways to see things and that someone else's ideas may be usefully incorporated into one's own thinking. Since there is no real right and wrong, I am neither right nor wrong and therefore changing my thoughts and ideas based on new information is less threatening.

I have painted this in glowing terms recognizing that it doesn't really operate that way in many cases. But the process above is a part of what has led to a world value called "tolerance." And if there is an absolute in the current worldview of right and wrong, it is that people must be tolerant of others and if people are not tolerant, they are wrong. Now this whole concept is fraught with problems, not the least of which is seen in how incredibly intolerant tolerance advocates are of people who believe in a Christian or other religious worldview that posits that there is a God that determines absolute truth. For example, stories of kids getting bad grades for writing about their faith in schools or being told that they can't talk about Jesus in their speeches for speech class or write about Jesus in their writing classes or draw pictures of Jesus in their art classes are common.

At the same time, tolerance has produced a more open attitude to the ideas, practices, and beliefs of people not like us and perhaps a greater willingness to be molded into another way of thinking than is often seen in church attenders. Christians in the media world are often portrayed as angry, hard, judgmental intolerants who are rightly judged by the tolerant world. And there are sufficient examples to fuel the news media's desire for evidence to support the characterization of Christians in general as being that way. Many years ago, I remember watching *60 Minutes* and my favorite part was always the commentary by Andy Rooney. I remember him saying once (along these lines), "I don't believe in abortion, but I like the people that are for it better than the people who are against it."

It is possible to be right about something and be so for the wrong reasons and in the wrong way. Perhaps what those of us who claim a Christian faith could do is to adopt the worldly value of "tolerance" in our relationship with Jesus! In tolerance, people are encouraged to hear and consider the opinions of others before coming to judgment or reacting emotionally based on their own pre-decided ideas. Maybe that's what James is talking about when he suggests that people should be "quick to listen and slow to become angry because a person's anger does not bring about the righteous life that God desires." (1:20) Once another's opinions are heard and considered, people are encouraged to find truth in those other opinions which can be incorporated into their own ideas and thoughts—in other words to actually change their opinions and attitudes and even practices based on what someone else believes. Maybe if I could become more "tolerant" of Jesus, I could become more like him and less like myself.

Have you seen the Christian bumper sticker that says, "God said it. I believe it. That settles it."? I like the idea of the message—there is a greater truth than my own and that I am going to submit to it. I believe that this rather blunt statement on the back of some cars somewhat accurately reflects the Genesis story. Tolerance people find this kind of thinking challenging at best, but more likely offensive. To tolerance people, a bumper sticker like this one really says, "I am not going to use my brain. I am going to follow my leader as if I were in a cult." In fact, tolerance people often see Christian churches, especially so-called conservative ones, as little better than cults and the kind of restrictive thinking reflected in the bumper sticker as the cause of all kinds of evil in the world from war to racism to wealth accumulation and so on. Of course, this takes us back to the intolerance of the tolerant, but that's not the point here.

I respect followers of Jesus who are able to convert the bumper sticker philosophy to real life living. However, I am not convinced that anyone, even committed followers who really know their bibles well, are ever able to actually do what the bumper sticker says. In fact, I think the bumper sticker would be a more accurate reflection of how things really work, if it said:

> "*I believe it.*
> *I found a place where God said it.*
> *(And others who share my belief about the meaning of this verse.)*
> *That settles it.*"

While we church folk can often acknowledge in words the idea of the Genesis story, at that subconscious level it seems that often our opinions and beliefs precede the God part. Instead, we often use God to justify our beliefs, which come from within our own understanding. Looked at this way, designations such as liberal or conservative lose their significance within the church as both tend toward following the parts of the scripture with which they are the most comfortable and gathering with others who identify with the same themes. Then, in order to prove their goodness, each looks at the groups of others who think differently and identify them as "wrong."

"Those people don't really follow Jesus because they don't (do what we do)."

It doesn't matter what the "do what we do" is, the process looks the same. Maybe it's that they don't give enough to the poor. Maybe it's that they don't focus on missions. Maybe it's that they don't oppose abortion. Maybe it's that they spend too much on their church building. Name the issue and the process is the same. We invoke God to justify our priorities which we often determine independent of God. Then we strengthen the goodness of our beliefs by pointing out how wrong others are.

For me, the saddest part of all of this is the brokenness that has resulted in the overall church body. Jesus gave his disciples the new command, "Love each other as I have loved you. By this all people will know you are my disciples; if you love each other." (John 13:35) When he was praying before he was arrested and crucified, he prayed that his followers would be one, as he and God were one (John 17:11). It doesn't take a very close look to see that the Christian church would have a hard time proving that it represents disciples of Jesus if this is the test! No wonder people outside the church can't quite figure out what this so-called "body of Christ" is all about!

But this process is universal. The tolerance people do it. Atheists do it. Everyone does it! If you look beyond the content to the process, people believe what they believe and then find quotes and writings of chosen "gods" who support what they believe. To strengthen the goodness of their beliefs, they find others who share them. Everyone who doesn't believe what the group believes is "wrong." (That settles it!) Sometimes we are able to dress up our judgment of the wrongness of others by saying that others who don't think like us are not yet "enlightened." In the end, they are still wrong until they agree with us.

All of this, both inside and outside the church, points to the same thing. People actually think that they know something; that we as individuals have the knowledge of good and evil. Our understanding of what is right is, by definition, good, since we think it is and we know what is good and what is evil. Since we are good, and therefore what we think on certain issues is right, those who do not think as we do are, by definition, wrong. We don't like to go to this point, but not only are they wrong, but they might be (whisper) "evil." The only point at which any kind of god enters the picture is when we need to justify our rights and wrongs by attributing them to a higher power who agrees with us (NOT with whom we agree as we like to say!).

Looked at in this way, almost every imaginable conflict from individual relationships to international relations can be seen to conform to this sequence. Radical Islam is doing the same thing that Chinese Communists are doing and that Israeli Jews and Palestinians are doing to each other and that Irish Protestants and Catholics do to each other and that the couple down the street that just got divorced are doing to each other. It looks different because the issues and context are different, but the foundation is the same. People are not good at their core, as the current worldview seems to think. People are prideful, self-centered, insecure, control freaks! Individually and corporately. And unless people are intentional about overcoming their personal opinion based thinking and decision-making, they will tend to help themselves and hurt others. *I* will tend to help ***myself*** and hurt others.

Looking for Jesus in All the Wrong Places

At the core of our created being is a longing for significance—for goodness. In the Genesis worldview, people are looking for what was lost at the moment of the Big Bite, when people suddenly knew that they were naked and for the first time, were ashamed. Ever since then people have been looking for something and we see it in the restlessness of our souls expressed in endless quests through the world of consumerism or political activism or revolving door relationships or mind altering substances or being good church people. People are looking for something that was lost.

In the Big Bite Theory, the key to understanding the search is coming to terms with our own individual and corporate brokenness. We have strayed from what we were created to be. We have wandered away directly as a result of our own brokenness and something "good" is needed to fix what is wrong; to restore what has been broken. The bible version of all this leads to a "savior, which is Christ the Lord," to quote the angels speaking to the shepherds (Luke 2:11). Jesus comes to restore the relationship with the Creator that was broken at the tree of the knowledge of good and evil and which people have been trying to reclaim ever since.

As a believer in Jesus, I believe that Jesus really is what (who) everyone is looking for. I also believe that the current worldview celebrating the goodness of people has confused the search in many ways. In order to "find" Jesus (a curious expression since I doubt that Jesus is lost), a person must experience his or her need for Jesus. But in the current worldview so common not only in the world but in the Christian church, we resist seeing the badness that is within us. We are supposed to be good people and the badness we see in ourselves is looked at as an anomaly—maybe it's something you ate for lunch. I think that well-meaning people have confused goodness with value and so have confused the searchers.

Individual human beings are the most precious, valuable thing on earth. But as we have noted through these pages, to say that people are "good" is to deny the bulk of the evidence of the effect of human decision making. Still, our faith in our goodness persists. And it colors our interpretation of what we see in ourselves and in others. The foundational belief that people are good is often, maybe almost always, operating below the level of consciousness. We don't even realize how much we interpret experiences from that perspective. As a result, we can be looking for something that is missing not even beginning to realize that what is missing is "goodness." Rather, the very goodness that is needed is assumed as a constant.

This is a pretty thick concept for me so let me see if by giving an example of how this operates I can make it more clear. I was talking recently with a young man who was struggling somewhat with his faith in Jesus. He was raised in a mainline type of church and attended public school through graduation. He came to a more personal faith during his freshman year of college and now that he was beginning his senior year, he had some concerns about faith and church and Jesus. His basic difficulty was that as he looked at the lives of people who claimed to follow Jesus, he didn't see that those people were acting the way he expected. He was questioning along these lines: "If Jesus (God) is real, why do people who claim to believe in him act this way?"

This seems to be a valid point of argument for many people today. And it has been advanced by no less than Gandhi who said, "I like your Christ. I do not like your Christians. They are so unlike your Christ." People are looking for something that is missing and one of the places where people look is religion and one of the people in religion that people look to is Jesus. Jesus is almost universally thought of as being a good person. So, the unconscious argument goes like this: "If good people follow a good Jesus, followers of Jesus should be good people." I know it sounds a bit circular and it is. The end (people who follow Jesus will be good) is also the beginning (people are good at their core). However, when searching people look at the representatives of Jesus, they see so many challenging behaviors and situations that the whole thing unravels.

But if the idea that people are basically good is assumed as true, the only part of the process that can be wrong is the Jesus part.

"He must not be who people say he is."
"The things in the bible must not be true, at least not today."

But what if the foundational thinking about people is what is wrong? What if people are not good at their core? My conversation with the young man led to this statement, "You will never see Jesus in his people. If you look for him there, you will be disappointed because followers of Jesus are still people." This sounds a bit counter (Christian) culture in a church world that says things like, "You may be the only Jesus someone ever meets." But do you know anyone who acts like Jesus 100% of the time? What would that even look like? How about 75% of the time? How would anyone know? This is one of those moments when what Jesus said to the rich young ruler who asked the "good teacher" what he needed to do to be saved seems clear to me:

"Why do you call me good? No one is good but God alone."
(Mark 10:18)

Jesus seems to be saying that being good is not a part of the human condition.

But being valuable is. As the young man protested that he had followed all the rules of the law his whole life, Jesus responded with one of my favorite lines in the whole bible:

"Jesus looked at him and loved him." (vs. 21)

Jesus looked right at this guy's biggest fault, but didn't judge him or reject him or despise him or ridicule him. He valued him. He loved him.

And then he told the young man the truth. "One thing you still lack." Jesus looked right into the heart of this young ruler and exposed the barrier this legalistically righteous man had built up in his own life. Jesus looked past the fool's good of following religious rules, of being good by human standards, and he showed the young man what was really in his heart—"Go and sell everything you have and give to the poor" (vs. 21). Now if the young ruler is good and the good teacher has given him good advice, wouldn't it follow that the young ruler would take the advice? Instead he goes away sad "because he had much wealth." His wealth had become greater than his goodness.

Like this young ruler of bible times, many people know that they are lacking something but are rejecting Jesus because he doesn't seem to be a good answer and they are basing that on the behavior of people who claim to follow Jesus. What I believe is that a person can see the EFFECTS of Jesus in a person's life, but that you can never see the fullness of the goodness of Jesus in individual human beings. People who follow Jesus still struggle with their inner pride, selfishness, and judgment. If a person looks for Jesus in another human and sees pride, selfishness, and judgment—and those character traits aren't hard for us judgmental folks to see in others—the almost inevitable conclusion for someone who is searching is to decide that Jesus is not real or not worth it. Not that someone called Jesus did not exist. Only, he wasn't the God/Savior/Redeemer of the bible.

So looking for Jesus in other people is often going to be a stumbling block to actually seeing him since even followers of Jesus are going to reveal their non-Jesus like character eventually. But I encounter an even more difficult problem in looking for Jesus in ourselves. I once heard a Unitarian Universalist say that in her way of believing, "We are all Jesus." I like UUs because they can believe just about anything—as long as it is positive. They are often good people who believe that people are good and look for the good in others. However, I find the general belief system to fall into the trap of "Who gets to decide what is good?" If each individual person is permitted to define his or her own belief system then how can anyone be wrong? Do we then not become our own God when we get to decide for ourselves what is good and what is not? And doesn't that sound like what happened in the garden with Adam and Eve in the Genesis version?

> "You will not surely die," the serpent said to the woman, "For God knows that when you eat of it your eyes will be opened and you will be like God, knowing good and evil." (Genesis 3:4,5)

Often, the universal is appealed to with the caveat that one can believe whatever one wants "as long as it doesn't hurt anyone else." But where does that universal come from if we are all deciding for ourselves what to believe? Why is that universal . . . universal? In the end, I suspect it is a universal because it makes us (the majority) feel good, which goes back to the emotional decision making about what is good and what is not.

But I also find that in many ways the Unitarians I know have the closest thing to a summary of the current worldview. It might be expressed like this: Everyone is basically good and badness can be overcome by believing and thinking good things. Jesus is a good example, maybe the best, of just how good a person can be. But in the current worldview, we can all be like Jesus. We can all be good, because we all ARE good. If we look deep inside, we can find our inner Jesus. Kids raised with this view of people then come to school where I get to meet them. And this is where I see the problem of looking for Jesus inside ourselves played out.

In truth, I suppose I meet few kids who are looking for Jesus in themselves. But I find that almost all kids are looking for meaning in themselves. As kids grow and become developmentally able to deal with increasingly more complex ideas, meaning of life questions become a part of the thought process. Where did I come from? Why am I here? What happens when I die? These are the three biggies that everyone deals with on some level and kids are starting to deal with these questions in real terms as they go through their teenage years.

If a foundation has been laid which says basically that people are good, and if that foundation is a part of the unconscious assumptions that a kid makes about the world, then a troublesome trap has been laid. When Jesus asks, "Why do you look at the speck of sawdust in your brother's eye, and pay no attention to the plank that is in your own eye?" (Matthew 7:3), I don't believe he is saying that one person's sin is worse than the guy he is looking at. After all, if this teaching applies to anyone, it applies to everyone including the guy with the plank *and* the guy with the speck. What I have always gotten from this teaching is that no matter how much I may know about the problems/faults/sins of another person, I know FAR more about my own. So when I see a speck on someone else's life, I am seeing only a small part of what that person is dealing with. But if I am honest with myself, I am aware of much more that is wrong with me than with the other guy. If I add up all the specks in my own life that I know about, I end up with a plank's worth of crap that I am not proud of and that gives me no rightful position from which to judge the few specks I may see in others.

It's important to note that the speck/plank teaching from Jesus follows closely one of the most quoted of Jesus' sayings: "Do not judge or you too will be judged" (7:1). In fact, this may be one of the most quoted of Jesus' teachings by non-followers of Jesus against those who claim to follow Jesus. I saw an editorial cartoon recently that invoked this verse. It showed a rather unpleasant, angry preacher standing in the pulpit saying, "We must obey all of God's laws," and he was holding up a quote condemning homosexuality. Behind the preacher were what looked like the hands of God holding a bigger sign, which read "Judge not that ye be not judged." The inescapable irony is that the cartoonist was himself judging the judgments of those he claimed were being judgmental. It's a pretty tough circle to get out of and one that makes this "Don't judge" and "Take care of your own plank" teaching very difficult to implement no matter how appealing it may seem on the surface.

So back to the kids. I have mentioned that we refer to kids as young adults and one of the ways that I see that term applying is that kids are simply less subtle at doing what adults have become proficient at doing. Adults become pretty good at seeing their planks and justifying them. But before some kids get to adult justifications, they fall into the trap laid by the "people are basically good" foundation. This trap happens because all of us are aware of our planks.

It works like this. There is the unconscious assumption put in the minds of many kids that is the foundation of their understanding of the basic nature of people. This unconscious assumption is that people are good, as we have said multiple times now! As kids get older, they become more aware of moral issues in terms of thought and deed. They readily identify the specks in the lives of others, but they are also aware of the plank in their own eye. Because of the assumption that people are good, the specks in others are viewed as exceptions to their natural goodness. But the internal planks are another thing.

In this little trap, kids are taught to see the specks in others and react to them by saying things like, "He's basically a good person, but . . . ." and then to identify the speck. But the specks are always exceptions to the stated rule—"He's basically a good person." Variations of this concept are heard in statements like, "She didn't really mean to hurt anyone." (People are good so their intent is usually also good.) And "He was just having a bad day." (Outside circumstances occasionally cause good people to act badly). These statements seem to satisfy the worldview of "people are basically good" by providing reasonable explanations for the badness that is seen in the behavior of others. This works well for dealing with the specks in others. But what is a kid to do with the planks in their own lives that they are faced with every day?

I have had many teenagers say to me in one way or another, "If you knew the bad things that I have inside of me, you would not think that I am a good person." (Of course, they don't know that I already don't think they are a good person—just a very valuable one!) When kids see the plank in their own eye, they almost do a reverse of what Jesus was talking about. Instead of ignoring the plank, they focus on and even obsess on it. They begin to believe that the plank in their eye represents a core of badness that is the exception to the goodness rule. "I see that other kids have faults and problems too (specks), but they are nothing compared to what is inside of me!" When kids get caught in this trap, they engage in a different kind of comparative judgment and their inner darkness collides with their foundational understanding that people are good. At that point, a teenager, or any person for that matter, has two choices. The first choice is to question and reconsider and even reform their basic understanding about the nature of people. However, this basic understanding is often so ingrained as to be assumed as a universal truth. It never occurs to most adults to question it, much less teenagers.

The second choice, and the one I see so many kids make, is to reach the conclusion that, "I am the exception to the rule. Most people are good, but I am the exception to the rule of goodness and know that I am, in fact, bad." Some of these kids become angry. Some become depressed. But some of them are among the kindest young people I know. They treat others well because they continue to believe that people are good and that others deserve to be treated well. But they treat themselves badly and often allow themselves to be treated badly all the while believing that they deserve it. It is a sad trap to see a kid get stuck in. If they were able to see that everyone has planks but you can only see your own plank and that the specks you see in others are specks because you can't see into their hearts and minds and their planks; in other words, if they could change their foundational thoughts about the goodness of people, they would be free to deal with their planks without the burden of thinking that they are worse than everyone else.

Not all kids go through this process, at least not to this extent. But many do, especially those coming from backgrounds that are more difficult. I believe kids would be so much better served if the foundational thoughts built in at an early age taught them that while they are the most valuable thing in the world, they will always struggle with a "dark side" that is present in every human being. This dark side causes people to act in ways that are selfish and judgmental and sometimes angry and mean. Then when the "evil" thoughts come, kids would not be surprised or think that there must be something wrong with them that is not wrong with everyone else they know. We give lip service to this concept by teaching kids that "everyone makes mistakes." But even as you hear yourself say it, you can hear the tone of voice that communicates that while everyone makes mistakes, mistakes are the exception to who we are at our core. In the Genesis view, mistakes are the expectation not the exception and overcoming our natural tendency to make mistakes is the goal and the victory. In the Genesis view, our value comes not from our performance compared to others but from our existence itself.

In the worst of cases, teenagers who fall into this trap of believing that they are the exception to the goodness rule come to the conclusion that the only reasonable thing to do is to take oneself out of the game—to commit suicide. These teens have lost any sense that they have or can have any value. They have tried everything they know how to do and have come up short. The Genesis view points to restoration and victory over darkness, but it also points to a reality that a person cannot do this on their own strength or knowledge or "goodness." It requires an outside relationship with someone who ascribes value to you regardless of your performance. Sometimes people can do this for each other in a limited way as we see in the inspirational stories of individual teenagers who point to a teacher or coach or other caring adult who gave their lives meaning. The ultimate fulfillment of this concept in the Genesis view is the restoring relationship with God through Jesus. According to the bible, "You were bought at a price." (1 Corinthians 6:20a). A price is what tells us how valuable something is. The universal price for every person was paid by Jesus, meaning that each person is worth $Jesus.00. This does not make us good. But it does make us the most valuable things in all of creation. How often I have wished that kids that I have worked with understood this.

The Most Important Resource?

Earlier I mentioned that I have the privilege of being involved in a poverty program in my hometown of Dubuque. I suppose it is better to say that it is an anti-poverty program. It is based on the work of Ruby Payne (www.ahaprocess.com) and her concepts for understanding poverty laid out in her books *A Framework for Understanding Poverty* and *Bridges Out of Poverty* (with Phil Devol and Terie Dreussi-Smith). We have also added a companion program known as the Circles Campaign from www.circlescampaign.org. I mention these programs as an introduction to this section so that if you are interested in this work, you can visit these websites and get more information.

One of the basic concepts that we deal with in the Bridges work involves the judgment that takes place when a person sees behavior in others that they do not understand. This is a universal experience of people that is in many ways the focus of this book! When we see behavior that we do not understand, we, as people, have to do something with the information. And the first instinct that people have is to judge the moral character of the person who is behaving in a way that does not make sense. In the divisions between economic classes in our culture, this results in one of the most common beliefs held by the middle class about people in poverty being that they are "lazy." The reasoning goes something like this, "Since people in poverty are not living the way that I do and since their lives are not successful (in my terms), there must be something wrong with them, some flaw in their character which has led to them living the way they do."

The assumptions that are made in just that one statement are worth much more exploration than we will do here, including the assumption that my way of life is good or better than theirs and the assumption that all that I have is the direct result of choices that I have made—in other words, the idea that there is a level playing field from the start with the only variable being effort and attitude. But for now, see how this concept reflects a worldview. Very rarely will those who think that people in poverty are lazy say that they are also "bad" people; only that they have a flaw that prevents them from being (watch this) "as good as I am." The standard is the middle class life that I am living and the people in poverty are being measured against that standard which is assumed to be "good."

It works in reverse too! Aside from the middle class myth about the laziness of the poor, there is also the image of the poor that comes from a sort of noble savage mindset that sees people in poverty as somehow more pure and even closer to God than those of us who are living in more financially stable situations. However, my ongoing work with people in poverty both in the schools I serve and in our community program has taught me that people in poverty are human, too! So, when middle class people see people in poverty acting in ways that don't make sense to them, the middle class people often conclude that people who are in poverty are "lazy." But when people in poverty see middle class people acting in ways that don't make sense to them, they say that middle class people are "Stuck up! All they care about is their money." It is the nature of human beings to judge those who are different as being morally flawed. Judgment of others as morally flawed gives us permission to continue to live as we do without considering our own flaws or how we might better understand others.

Dr. Payne identifies eight resources that are a part of a sustainable life, of which financial is only one. One of the eight is the spiritual resource. How much does a person believe that their life has meaning beyond current circumstances or that there exists a higher power that will give a person strength to make it through difficult times? Spiritual resources can be a great asset when times are hard. I have found that many people in poverty have strong spiritual lives. For those who believe in God, they have an understanding of their desperate need for

God on a daily basis that many middle class people never understand. After all, middle class folk like me earned our food and house and car and so on. I have summarized it this way: When it comes to active spirituality, middle class people are often religious but not always spiritual (think church attendance, proper attire, serving on committees, etc.); whereas people in poverty are more often spiritual but not always religious (think dress, language, habits, etc.).

At one of our weekly meetings, we were having a discussion about spiritual resources. These meetings involve people in middle class and poverty working together to break down barriers of misunderstanding. As we talked about spirituality in general and how to know if a person is strong in spirituality or weak, it was astutely pointed out by one of the people that everyone has a spirituality. It may be completely unconscious but everyone has some framework by which they interpret life's events and life in general; an understanding of the meaning of life so to speak. Even atheists have an explanation for the way things are and an understanding of the way things should be. It may not involve a god at all, but it remains the context in which they understand and explain their world.

In many ways, the most common use of spirituality is to define what is good and what is not. This is defined based on the basic understanding of what life is all about which is what our inner spirituality does for us. It seems that far too often we allow our behaviors to influence our explanations. In other words, if there is some opinion or behavior that we value, we will find ways to make it conform to our inner spirituality by adjusting the spirituality rather than the behavior! (Similar to the Should Do/Do Do circles.) But in the process of working this out, people are almost universally trying to reach a place where their outer behavior and inner beliefs match and both are "good." In the process, we meet people whose behaviors are not like ours and since we are "good," what they are doing must be "bad." The result of this is that often people's spirituality is used to beat up others, at least in terms of judgment, while using the judged badness of others to reinforce our own goodness.

During our group discussion, we looked at some selections from the book of Proverbs in the bible, all of which dealt with poverty. Here are two that represented differing views of the issue:

"Lazy hands make a man poor, but diligent hands bring wealth." (10:4)

"Speak up for those who cannot speak for themselves, for the rights of all who are destitute. Speak up and judge fairly; defend the rights of the poor and needy." (31:9)

It was easy to see that many of the proverbs we looked at addressed poverty from differing perspectives, so we talked about which ones were our favorites. As we moved through the discussion, it was also easy to see that the proverbs that most appeal to us are the ones that best match what we already think about poverty. If we are inclined to think that people in poverty need to take action to get themselves out of poverty, we tend to favor those like the first proverb above. On the other hand, if we tend to view poverty as resulting from systemic issues and economic injustice, we tend to favor those proverbs more like the second.

But both of these proverbs are in the bible. Is one more right than the other? For those who accept the bible as at least inspired by God, they can't easily dismiss the proverbs that don't favor their own point of view. But that is just what it seems that so many people do with their spirituality. They take the parts that they like and that fit with their own perceptions of right and wrong and use those to support and prove their beliefs. In this context, they memorize all the proverbs that support their already held views. Then often those proverbs are used to judge others who are different than themselves as being less good. This tends to be a fairly shallow and self-centered kind of spirituality to be blunt. And it is difficult to grow in understanding of oneself or of others operating from this point of view. We don't need to grow when we think like this because not only do we know what is right and good, but we even have scripture to back it up!

What I have been learning lately is that it is much more useful for me to spend time reflecting on the proverbs that aren't as easy for me to agree with or understand. I can already see what the proverbs I like mean because they agree with what I already believe. But a deeper spirituality takes place when I allow some concept that is hard for me to understand to change what I believe rather than to only believe what is easy for me. It's true with the proverbs and with everything I read in the bible. The bible gives me a small glimpse into the thinking of God, if I believe that the bible is inspired. When I encounter things in the bible that aren't easy for me, I can either decide that God is wrong or question my own understanding as possibly being out of line with God. One makes me change to conform to God, one requires God to conform to my thinking. One leads to growth, one to stubbornness!

Here is what we decided at our discussion about spirituality. First, we decided that perhaps spirituality is the most important resource because even if you don't think you have a spirituality, your understanding of the meaning of life is a part of every decision you make. Second, we decided that spirituality should not be used to prove "what's wrong with you," but instead should always ask, "What's wrong with me?" When we use our spirituality to define others, we are engaging in fool's good thinking since we can only see what is on the surface. When we use our spirituality to understand ourselves better, we engage in the refining process that helps us to better reflect the real value that God has placed in each one of us.

Taking Sides

Have you noticed that in every discussion there are sides? This is true from the beginnings of social conversations in pre-school and continues through extensive and profound discussions about politics, economics, religion, and other "grown up" subjects. Some people are more prone to taking sides than others, but everyone is inclined toward taking sides. And sometimes what is important is not what side a person is on, but that they are on a side.

We recently had a difficult transition in my son's soccer club in which the director of the club and the board came to a mutual conclusion that it would be better to not renew the director's contract. There were a lot of issues involved with the decision but one of them, although not spoken, was that he was the first paid director the club had employed and as such had brought in change. Change is always hard whether it is good change or bad change. There were many people in the club who passionately supported the director and many were almost as passionate in their opposition of the director. It boiled down to this: the people that loved him were those whose kids had him as a coach for their team. The ones who loathed him were those whose kids did not have him for a coach.

When the decision was reached to end the relationship, an open meeting was held for parents to hear what was happening and to have an opportunity to express their feelings. As with any politically and emotionally charged situation, a lot of people showed up. Most of those who came to the meeting expressed their "side" of the story in a rational, if occasionally emotional, manner. However, there were a few on both sides of the argument who frankly seemed to relish the conflict. They expressed their side with emotion that seemed devoid of reason. As is often the case, those who expressed themselves in this way occasionally resorted to mild profanity and name calling and even indirect threats to take actions against the club to prove their point. Some were visibly shaking as they expressed their "opinions" (translate—emotions)

Here is what occurred to me after the meeting was over. I firmly believe that if the "lovers" had not had the director for a coach and if the "haters" had had the director for a coach, the exact same meeting would have taken place and the exact same people would have shown up and they would have expressed themselves in the exact same way—except they would have taken the opposite sides! In other words, the content of the arguments of the emotional people involved did not matter—they were there to emote in support of their passionate conviction that what they think is right—is right! Some people are inclined to passionately (emotionally) argue their point regardless of what their point is!

This to me was a great example of what happens when we allow emotions to control our thinking, or perhaps more accurately, to take priority over our thinking. We have all seen people in an emotional state in an argument where there is no reasoning with them. There is little rational thought taking place in that moment. In this process, the "rightness" of the argument is assumed since "I know what is right because I know good and bad and this makes me feel good (or bad)." The foundation of our position is not our rational thinking, but how the current situation makes us feel. Good people feel good and know what good is because of how it makes them feel. When something makes them feel bad, it must be wrong! And, as in the case of the meeting I was at, if someone dares to express an opinion contrary to theirs or make a decision contrary to their understanding of what is right, an emotional reaction is justified. It becomes, in fact, "right" to bully people with emotion and name-calling and threats. In the meeting I mentioned above, the situation of "justification by emotion" was evident in that this was a scheduled meeting. There was nothing spontaneous about the emotions that were expressed. These were premeditated "tantrums"—some people even had notes!

Premeditated AND coordinated. Certain groups of people arrived together, sat together, and debriefed together after the meeting in the lobby of the building where the meeting took place. I also understand that there was plenty of pre-meeting contact via phone and e-mail—folks jockeying for position, so to speak! It isn't enough for us to know that we are on the right side—we have a real need to make sure others agree with us. And not only must they agree with us, but they also must agree about a) who is wrong, and b) the moral failings of the wrong. We go after the character of those who are in the wrong camp. We question their motivation, their selfishness, their mean spirit—we question their goodness. I suppose it's better not to say that we question those who are wrong; we just flat out judge them!

But it's more than that. At our worst, we really do bully them. In fact, this whole process reminds me of a scene I see every day in the schools where I work. Groups of people gathering together—intentionally including those who are like-minded and intentionally leaving out, rejecting, and sometimes mocking those who are judged as different. The difference is that in my work, those groups of people are usually junior and senior high school kids and at the soccer meeting, they were adults. We sometimes refer to teenagers as "young adults" and perhaps they are. But if that's true, then it seems to me that many if not most or even all adults are just as accurately described as "old teenagers." In so many cases, we adults do the same things to each other that teenagers do to each other—we are just better at justifying it. We're more subtle. Practice makes perfect!

When people talk about bullying and peer pressure and social exclusion among teenagers, one of the principles of the process is that in an attempt to deal with identity insecurity, teens will often group together and define their group by who is NOT included. In more casual terms, it is important to be cool and teens know who is cool by who is in their group and, sometimes more importantly, who is not in their group. Now cool can be defined in many ways and some teens will insist that they are not "cool." However, even among these "uncool" kids, their group of friends typically like who they are and don't like who others are. This has been going on probably since forever in some form or other. But too often people today think that this is a teen problem. It's not. It's a human problem and it is directly related to a fool's good understanding of what is good and evil, right and wrong.

And here is what I think is kind of going on. Deep inside—even deeper than the knowledge of good and evil—there is a nagging insecurity that we really don't know if we are right and good or not. Nor are we sure how to know for sure! To avoid dealing with this deeper question, people surround themselves with people who are like them in order to affirm that their impressions of right and wrong are, in fact, right! People take comfort in belonging to a group of like-minded people. When teenagers do it, we call it "peer pressure" and we tell them not to do it. We say things to these young adults like: "Find other friends," and "Learn to hang out with people who are different than you," and, "If your friends jumped off a bridge . . . ."—you get the idea.

But when adults do essentially the same thing by joining churches or clubs or causes or whatever lines up with their interests and comforts, we call it "personal choice" and we affirm our right to it. One of my personal favorites, as I mentioned earlier, is hearing adults talk about groups they belong to in words like, "I really like this group because we are not judgmental." In so many ways, we really are just old teenagers.

But it doesn't work, does it? Eventually, we find ourselves alone with our ideas of right and wrong and our doubts about what we really do know. Eventually we have to face the deeper questions of where (or from whom) right and wrong come from. Eventually we have only ourselves and our morality. Look at this illustration of how it all closes in on us.

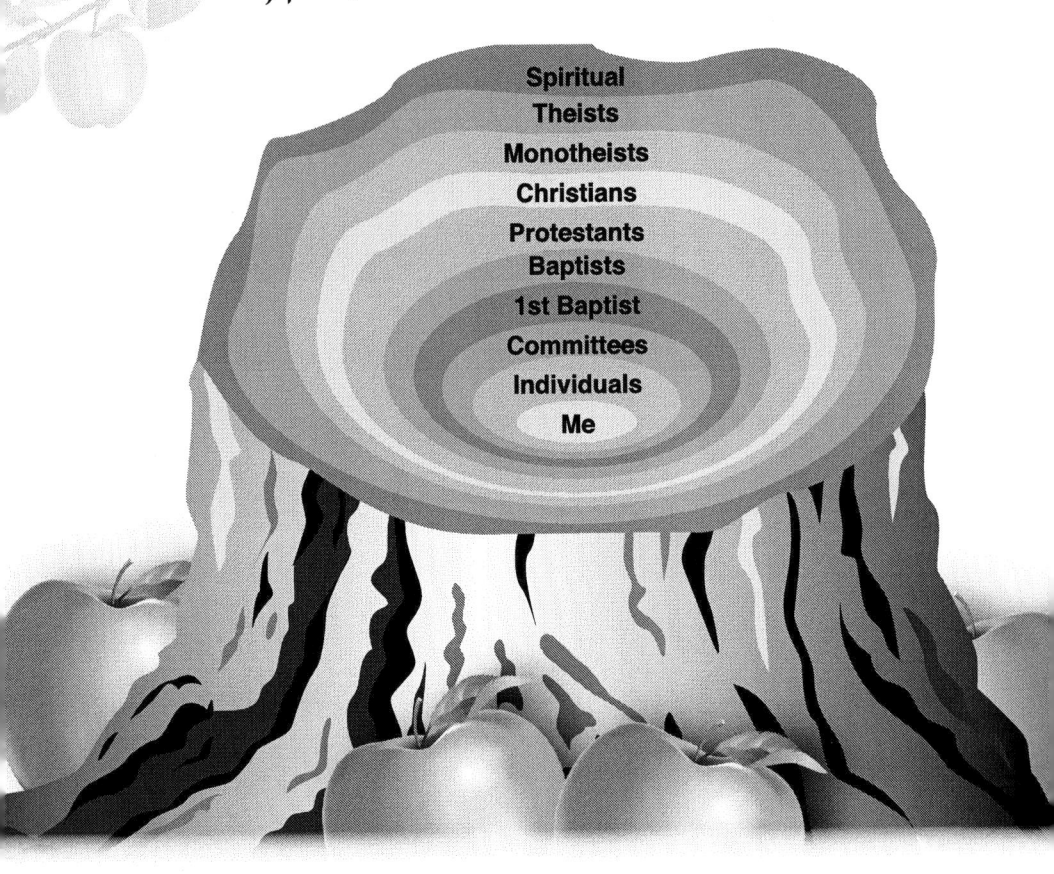

Spiritual
Theists
Monotheists
Christians
Protestants
Baptists
1st Baptist
Committees
Individuals
Me

The concentric circles represent groups of which we are a member. Because of our natural tendency to judge those who are not like us, we look from inside each circle and judge those on the outside of that circle. So for a typical white, male, middle class Protestant like me it goes like this. The largest circle represents people who are spiritual and believe that there is something spiritual beyond what we can see and touch. These are people of faith—any faith—anyone who believes that there is something spiritual beyond us. In this circle, I may find all kinds of strange beliefs when compared to my perspective, but we can agree that the naturalists and atheists who say that there is no spiritual world (those outside the big circle) are nuts.

The next circle includes those who have some form of theistic belief, that is, that there is a god or many gods or some kind of supreme being or beings. In this circle, I agree with the Hindus, with many gods, but not with the Buddhists. I'd even agree with those who believe in Greek, Roman or Norse gods.

Then comes a tighter circle, which represents people who have a monotheistic faith; that is they believe in a single God who is responsible for all existence. In this circle, I might find myself in agreement with people of Jewish or Muslim faith and we might easily find ourselves agreeing that those outside of our circle (e.g., Hindus, Buddhists, Pagans, etc. as well as the aforementioned atheists) are in for a big surprise when they find out the truth. "What are they thinking to believe in reincarnation!?" or some such questions are asked to affirm our good beliefs and their bad ones.

The next circle is the Christian circle. Now I'm comfortable with other Christians but have to sit in a bit of judgment on the Jews and Muslims who are now outside my circle. Then comes the Protestant circle and out go the Catholic and Orthodox Christians. Next is the denominational circle. Since I attend a Baptist church, I now can judge some of the silly things I see in other denominations and chuckle about them knowingly with my Baptist friends who completely understand and agree with my point of view. Infant baptism versus believer's baptism would be a good example here!

Now I have a circle, which includes my own church. Those of us who attend our church obviously have made the decision to do so because it is better than other alternatives that are available including other Baptist churches in town. But it doesn't stop there. First, there are committees (an almost universal evil in my view!). The worship committee knows for sure that their priorities are more important than the missions committee. Meanwhile, the finance committee knows that they get the final say anyway! Then there is the individuals circle. In my own church, there are people who see things my way and those that don't. (Any politics in YOUR church?) So now, I have a small circle of people who affirm my ideas of right and wrong, and a whole lot of people outside the various circles who do not. And then I start looking at those few people left and I begin to realize that they aren't so great either!

And I find myself alone, wondering if this is really the way it is supposed to be. Is what I think really right? Am I really good? This can be a very lonely place and one often avoided by people.

Draw your own circles. It works for jobs and schools and hobbies and sports and political parties. But it all leads to the same place. We are at the center of a process that eventually traps us in our own judgments and we are alone. Do we really know so much after all? Are we really so sure that our knowledge of good and evil is accurate? And when we get to this point, it seems that we have two choices. We can ignore the questions and build up our defenses. We can strengthen our relationships with those most like us and affirm our belonging based on common understandings and values. We can become really good at being adults who never stopped dealing with people like we did as teenagers.

The second choice is to open up a real self-examination. When we do this and see our own natural tendencies toward judgment of others, we have an opportunity to grow immeasurably in our ability to relate to, accept, and love those who are different than us. Judgment is natural. Anyone can do it and left to our own unexamined life we all will. To not judge must be an intentional decision to overcome the natural. But this decision to not judge does not come through understanding others, but through understanding ourselves. This is inconsistent with the world's teaching right now.

In our world, and I see this all the time and in many forms at school, the common teaching is that we should seek to understand how others are different than we are, because all people are basically good and have good things about them. This idea makes sense on the surface. But, of course, that's where the fool's good is. If we see the good in others, then we will be more tolerant and accepting. Since we all want to be tolerant, this will work, right? Assuming that we are all motivated to be tolerant, this might be right. Many people are intellectually motivated to be tolerant, but haven't dealt with their own natural tendency to be NOT tolerant. Maybe it helps to look at the word itself.

One can only be *tolerant* of something with which they do not agree or which makes them uncomfortable. It takes no talent to be tolerant of my friends. But I have to choose to be tolerant of their irritating habits. I am not tolerant when I have a nice cup of coffee. I have to be tolerant when I take that nasty stuff a person drinks before a colonoscopy. In fact, I have to be tolerant of the whole colonoscopy process! You "tolerate" things you don't like.

This doesn't fit well with the world's view of tolerance. In today's teaching, tolerance has come to be code for "acceptance and approval." So if a person happens to be able to tolerate difference while at the same time not approving of it, they are considered to have failed the tolerance test and judged as intolerant. There is, in fact, no tolerance in our world for those who are deemed intolerant! In some ways, the only sin that our current culture recognizes is the sin of intolerance.

This intolerance of the intolerant seems to come from an unstated understanding that people are good and good people are tolerant. The problem from a Genesis worldview is that people are not good and are naturally intolerant of others who are not good by the judger's standards. The solution from a Genesis worldview is not to avoid real tolerance by becoming accepting of everything and everyone. Rather, by understanding the deeper truth of our own judgmental nature and choosing to become truly tolerant of those who are different than we are, we can begin to relate to others with genuine affection. To love as Jesus loved is not to say that everyone is okay, but to say that in spite of the fact that people are not okay, I will love them and serve them in any way that I can that honors God and cherishes the inherent value of each person. In my faith, Jesus tolerated the cross for my sin. I know WAY more about my sin than I ever will know about the sins of any other person on earth. In following Jesus' example (to love as I have been loved), I should be able to tolerate differences in other's beliefs and behaviors without compromising the standards that I claim.

Kids aren't really taught this at school. More or less, they are taught that it is good to tolerate (accept) others even if they are really different than you and that if you don't accept others exactly as they are, then you are intolerant or even bad. This creates a lot of tension in the inner thoughts of many young adults who know what many adults have forgotten: that they are judgmental and even kind of mean at their core. They work hard to be good (accepting) on the surface, but inside they struggle with their own deep, inner circle thoughts and wonder what is wrong with them, as I mentioned before.

Another form that I see this take in what passes for moral instruction in our culture today comes in the form of what we used to call Values Clarification. It has other names and forms today, but it has its roots in the old Values Clarification material. In this process, kids are taught that they need to decide what they believe and learn to understand that others may believe differently than they do. While well intentioned, as most things are, this process leads kids and eventually full-grown adults right back into themselves where they are responsible for their own definitions of good and evil. They can't depend on some established standard. Instead, they must clarify their own values and establish their own standards.

Now while this process of clarifying one's own values is being taught, make no mistake that the system is clearly trying to impart some values. Whatever program is being used, words like honesty, kindness, responsibility, tolerance, and so on are being included in the list of values the kids are supposed to clarify in themselves. Also included is the idea that you have to make up your own mind, think for yourself, and don't do what your friends do just because they are your friends (back to peer pressure!). This gets kind of sticky to work through with abstract concepts like responsibility and tolerance, but it becomes more clear with concrete examples of teaching kids to think for themselves and expecting them to then make "good" decisions. My personal favorite is the "Just Say No" type anti-tobacco, alcohol, and drug use programs.

These programs are started at early grades in the schools and the basic approach is to teach kids early that there are good reasons not to smoke (or drink or do drugs) and no real good reasons to smoke. The kids are taught to make a figurative list (sometimes literal) of pros and cons of smoking. Ask any first grader who has been through this kind of teaching and they will likely be able to give you several reasons why smoking is bad for you and maybe one or none why someone might smoke. The one reason will be "to be cool." But first graders don't see other first graders who smoke as cool. So that reason isn't appealing. Recognizing that there are unique situations out there, in general there are very few first graders who are going to smoke or drink or do drugs. Teaching them reasons why not to do those things is pretty much meaningless. But teaching them how to think about these issues and make their own decisions is laying a pretty big trap for adolescence.

All through elementary school, Julie has been taught to think for herself and to make up her own mind. She graduated from the DARE program in sixth grade and now has gone on to junior high school. When Julie was in elementary school, she made a list just as she had been taught about why she was never going to start smoking. It kind of looked like this:

Smoking

Pros
1. Some people think it's cool.

Cons
1. You can get cancer.
2. It makes your clothes smell bad.
3. It costs lots of money.
4. My parents will be mad at me.
5. You could die.
6. It's against the law.
7. My teachers will be sad.
8. It makes your teeth yellow.
9. It makes your breath stink.

This pro/con list made it easy for Julie to see why she would never smoke. The cons clearly outweighed the pros. Of course, Julie had little opportunity to test her list in elementary school as she was never actually offered a cigarette by anyone, including any of her friends. Nor was she in any way interested in finding out what smoking was like.

But now Julie is in junior high and things have changed a bit. Some of her friends have started dabbling in various things they all said they would not do when they were learning about them during Red Ribbon Week in elementary school. Julie has even gone to a couple of parties where some of the people she knows have been smoking. Time to get out the list to see if the cons still outweigh the pros. Julie has been well taught to think for herself and not just to do what her friends are doing. In fact, in many cases, Julie has learned to not even do what her parents say just because they are her parents. She knows how to clarify her own values and she can make her own decisions; except now, the list looks like this:

Smoking

Pros

1. Some people think it's cool.

Cons

1. You can get cancer.
2. It makes your clothes smell bad.
3. It costs lots of money.
4. My parents will be mad at me.
5. You could die.
6. It's against the law.
7. My teachers will be sad.
8. It makes your teeth yellow.
9. It makes your breath stink.

So now, when Julie gets out the scale and weighs the decision, which side weighs more? And so, like many kids who in first and second grade swore they would never smoke (as if kids that age can make decisions like that!), Julie now joins those with clarified values who choose to do what they said they never would. And it's not even that the content has changed in the list of pros and cons; only the relevance of the content.

If this is true for smoking, it's the same for drugs and sex and shoplifting and lying to parents and other adults and cheating and all sorts of things that many of us, left entirely to our own "goodness," would do! What kids learn from this kind of instruction is not useful for making decisions that will affect their lives in a positive way (not smoking, not doing drugs, etc.). Instead, it teaches them a way of thinking that in many ways actually gives them permission to do the very things we thought we were teaching them not to do! We've taught them to think for themselves according their own knowledge of good and evil regardless of what their friends, teachers, or even their parents think.

What's missing in this discussion is a concept of things being right and wrong according to a standard that has nothing to do with what one thinks or feels based on a personal internal compass of good and evil. In the Genesis worldview, Adam and Eve did nothing wrong until they started deciding for themselves what was right and wrong. Then it was a disaster and we have all become a part of this disastrous way of thinking. In the book of Judges, it talks about chaos in Israel and it says, "In those days, Israel had no king, and everyone did as they saw fit." (Judges 21:25). That's just in case you are one of those folk who think that this problem just started in the 21st century! Or even the 20th century. This is a for-all-time human problem.

Julie, you should not smoke because it is wrong. Sure, there are lots of reasons why it makes sense that it would be wrong. But the fact that we can make sense out of why it is wrong has nothing to do with whether or not it is actually wrong. Even if you don't agree with any of these reasons, it's still wrong.

Now, I'm messing with folks who smoke and I know that. It is clear that people started smoking and continue to smoke for all sorts of reasons, including the "lesser of two evils" situation (It's better to smoke than gain weight, or do drugs, or be emotionally out of control, etc.). And the beginning of smoking is going to be hard to trace in human history. But somewhere back in the day, people discovered this "drug" that made them feel good. And as we know, anything that makes us feel good must BE good! Tobacco (nicotine) is a legal drug. But that does not make it any less a drug on which people become dependent to the point of addiction, often resulting in financial, emotional, and physical hardships for individuals and families and indeed our entire culture through health care and related costs.

But let's say that you don't agree that smoking is wrong; just plain wrong regardless of individual or government opinion. What about smoking illegal drugs? What about intravenous drugs? What about drugs a guy drops in some girl's drink so he can take advantage of her? What about rape in general? Are there any lines? Or is everything a list of pros and cons that an individual can make and then decide for him or herself?

At this point, someone thinks, some of those things are okay as long as you don't hurt anyone else. Without going into detail about how all sorts of behaviors can hurt others in various ways (If a teenager breaks his mom's heart by coming home drunk from a party at which no one got physically hurt, was anyone hurt?), the "as long as no one gets hurt" line in the sand is still a line in the sand. If you agree that there is a line, then the debate changes from whether or not people can make up their own minds to where the line is drawn and who drew it.

The Genesis worldview says that there is an ultimate authority to which we are all accountable. When people followed that authority, everything was cool. As soon as we started drawing our own lines, it pretty much all went to hell. The more prevalent cultural worldview of today is that each person can make up his or her own lines and no one can tell that person that he or she is wrong. As we have talked about all along, taken to its logical conclusion, no one's opinions, behaviors, attitudes, and choices, can ever be described as wrong—no matter how wrong they are! The introduction of an absolute line ("As long as no one gets hurt.") requires the introduction of a source of that line.

Kids are not taught about this in values clarification exercises and character education programs. They could be and so-called character education could be useful in exploring the lines that are out there. But we can't do that in schools these days—too close to religion. So the kids are left obeying teachers and other school authorities because they have to. And sometimes not obeying them saying, "You are not the boss of me. You can't tell me what to do." At the logical end of the world's worldview perspective, they're right.

An Application from Psalm 15

In our congregation, we spent a year going through the Psalms—not all of them but one for each Sunday of the traditional Sunday School year. When we got to Psalm 15, it brought up the whole "Who do we think we are?" deal to me again. Here is Psalm 15 from the NIV:

Lord, who may dwell in your sanctuary?
  Who may live on your holy hill?
He whose walk is blameless
  and who does what is righteous,
who speaks the truth from his heart
  and has no slander on his tongue,
who does his neighbor no wrong
  and casts no slur on his fellowman
who despises a vile man
  but honors those who fear the Lord
who keeps his oath
  even when it hurts
who lends his money without usury
  and does not accept a bribe against the innocent.
He who does these things will never be shaken.

The Psalm gives us a great list of criteria for who is "in" and who is "not in!" In the discussions in which I participated surrounding Psalm 15, it became quickly apparent to me, and to others as well, that our natural tendency is to read a psalm like this from the point of view that we are already in God's sanctuary; we're already living on God's holy hill. We may not be there physically but we know we will be there. And we know that we will be there because we don't do any of this stuff listed in the psalm. More than that, we know people who do and they will not be in God's sanctuary if the don't make some pretty significant changes!

Part of problem here is that we define the terms ourselves so that we do not get caught up in them! For example, when reading verse 2, how does one define "blameless" and "righteous?" My experience with people tells me that we first avoid definitions through the use of false humility (never spoken of with favor in the bible!). "I'm just a sinner saved by grace! I'm certainly not righteous or blameless!" And then some form of "I may not be perfect, but I'm doing the best I can and I'm basically a good person"—there's that word again. So who are those who are REALLY not blameless and not righteous? It ends up being a list of people who are not like me. I identify activities that I would never do. Then I find bible verses that support the idea that those actions are bad. And then I judge those who do what I have defined as unrighteous.

Verse 3—"no slander on his tongue; does his neighbor no wrong; casts no slur on his fellowman"? Who can claim this? And yet we do. We define "slander" to cover something other than what we do when we are talking about the people at our jobs or our pastor or the neighbor's kids or the new family down the street with the big, unruly dog. When we talk about these things, we are merely sharing information or comparing notes. When it comes to real slander, we remain blameless, of course.

Do we keep our oath "even when hurts" (v. 4)? I can't speak for anyone else, but I can say that I have made all kinds of commitments that I didn't keep even when it was easy! For me, it is more accurate to say that I will keep my oath "as long as I remember, and it isn't inconvenient!" But we define "oath" to be some major commitment, probably involving legal papers. Of course, I pay my bills, including my mortgage, so I keep my oaths for sure! I'm blameless in this area. As for all those people I told I would pray for them? That wasn't exactly an oath.

"And does not accept a bribe against the innocent." (v. 5) Now this one is easy because I am confident that I have never done this. In fact,

An Application from Psalm 15

I don't think anyone has ever even offered me a bribe against the innocent, at least not as I define bribery. I'm clear on this one. Of course, I have shopped at big box stores rather than at local merchants because it's cheaper to shop at those stores even though it may contribute to local merchants going out of business and the perpetuation of low wage part time jobs without benefits that trap people in an unsustainable economic lifestyle. And then there is the possible exploitation of really low wage earners in other countries. Have I been bribed by low prices?

When we read scripture and then speak definitions into it rather than letting scripture define us, we almost always default to our tendency to believe that we are good. We put ourselves in the sweet spot of blamelessness while acknowledging with words that, of course, no one is really blameless before God. The unspoken is always, "but I'm a lot more blameless than those guys!"

So who meets the Psalm 15 criteria? Who is it that "can never be shaken?" In the end, at least according to my understanding, only one has ever actually met these requirements. Only one is truly righteous and blameless. And if that is true, then I have a lot more in common with those who I see as unrighteous than I do with the God whose righteousness I sometimes claim as my own. Why am I so eager to judge others into the category of Not Like Me? I think it is because if they are not like me, then I can convince myself that I am better than I know that I am if I am really honest with myself. I am pretty sure, having worked with lots of people for lots of years, that we really do know that we are not that good. But it is SO hard to look at it for real and deal with it. By defining the terms ourselves, we can identify those that don't measure up and cushion ourselves from having honest moments that allow us to experience real purification that leads to discovering the real gold that exists within the human soul.

Would there not be a huge difference in the realm of human relationships if we were all not in the business of defining ourselves by the ungoodness of others? In Romans 14:4, it says, "Who are you to judge someone else's servant? To his own master he stands or falls. And he will stand, for the Lord is able to make him stand." What if we really lived by this? It's easy to do with people who are basically just like me. There might be a couple of things that bother me about them, but I can leave that for them to work out. But what if I could do it with those whose lives are completely different than mine?

Recently, I had an opportunity to speak to a community organization that addresses the needs of people with HIV/AIDS. Their clientele was certainly diverse economically, racially, and in terms of sexual orientation. This was not a traditional church crowd. But there is real compassionate work going on in this group. And there are real, precious human beings who feel rejected by the culture as a whole, and often by their own families. How can I, or anyone, best represent God in this situation?

Judgment and Preaching

I have determined that you need to meet my criteria of righteousness or . . .

Compassion and Preaching

I have determined that I am not your judge and master and will allow you to work out your issues with the real master. In the meantime, I will serve you with kindness and gentleness because we are both in the same boat.

Which of these is most likely to result in positive outcomes for others? For that matter, which is the most likely to result in positive outcomes for me? The first seems leads to an ever-hardening self-righteousness defined by the exclusion of others. The second leads to a deepening self-examination in which I discover more about my own brokenness while forming relationships that can help me while also providing an opportunity for me to "love as I have been loved." However, the first is easy and natural, while the second has to be intentional and can at times be painful.

The easiest, safest thing to do is to gather with others who share our judgments and opinions and define ourselves as much by those who are not a part of our group as by those who are. We reveal ourselves to be "old teenagers" again! And it happens naturally among people regardless of the issue; whether it is not serving people who are HIV Positive because HIV/AIDS is a marker of sin or rejecting all organized religion because the people who participate in organized religion are all hypocrites. We are all the same in this process of finding places of comfort where our judgments and opinions are confirmed often at the expense of others and almost always at the expense of opportunities for us to grow emotionally and spiritually.

The Fool's Road

Thinking of this concept of fool's good has given me a new appreciation for the wisdom of the Proverbs on the subject of being a fool. My own understanding of a fool in the context of the Proverbs is a person who has truth available to him, but chooses not to act according to that truth. I suppose we all do this at one time or another. "Sure, I'll have a third piece of that pie!" "I've got plenty of time—April 15th is still a week away!" "I'm pretty sure that girl smiled at me!" That sort of thing. A very long time ago, Solomon and/or some other Hebrew scholars saw this coming! Here are some nice examples. What I learned from looking at these is that I know why these are true but far too often, I act not according to what I know, but according to what I feel. It's the should do, do do thing again. See what you think. (These versions of the Proverbs are from the NIV and so use man/he/him etc. I feel more comfortable talking about what fools men are since I am one! I'm guessing these apply equally well across the gender divide!)

> *Whoever loves discipline loves knowledge, but he who hates correction is stupid—12:1*
> *The way of a fool seems right to him, but a wise man listens to advice—12:15*
> *A rebuke impresses a man of discernment more than a hundred lashes a fool—17:10*

I don't think any of us are particularly fond of being corrected or disciplined. We have more of a tendency to like being right and telling others who are wrong why we are right! I work with children for a living and can say with confidence that many of the children with whom I have the privilege to work would have much more sane and stable lives if they understood and applied the wisdom in these proverbs. But they are kids! How many adults are like this? When people encounter discipline and correction whether from an obvious source such as a boss or spouse, or from natural consequences of their actions, far too many times, instead of taking a step back and asking good questions and looking for lessons to be learned, people dig in their heels and get defensive. Rather than learn, we harden ourselves. Then someone who knows our situation and can see more objectively comes to us with a word of advice? "Thanks but no thanks. I know what I'm doing. My way is right." Or worse than a word of advice, someone comes to us with a rebuke! "Who are you to tell me what to do? You aren't so perfect yourself you know!" I don't know about you, but I've been foolish like this many times!

> *Even a fool is thought wise if he keeps silent and discerning if he holds his tongue—17:28*
> *A fool finds no pleasure in understanding but delights in airing his own opinions—18:2*
> *A fool's lips bring him strife and his mouth invites a beating—18:6*

In the category of talking too much, you talk too much! So do I, of course! I can't even read these three proverbs without feeling convicted. I am a talker and have to be intentional to keep my mouth shut. In my case, (read with sarcasm!) I talk a lot because I am so smart and everything I have to say is both more important and more insightful than whatever the person I am not really listening to is saying. I think I covered all three proverbs in that statement! I haven't actually ever received the beating that I invited, but I have seen the look in the eyes of those who wish they could have given me what I was asking for!

Listening really is an art and skill that requires practice and application. Or perhaps it is better said that listening takes practice in situations in which we don't really want to listen! For those of you who have done so, remember falling in love? It wasn't so hard to listen then was it? But for those of you who fell in love years ago and now have been listening to the same person for 20 years or so—is it still so easy? Many long time couples will say that the habit of listening to the same person makes it easier to not listen because we start to know what the other person is going to say before they say it—or at least we think we know!

Have you had the privilege of having a discussion with someone who disagrees with you on some issue that is very important to you? Do we as people tend to listen well when emotions are running high? It seems that we spend more time thinking about the next brilliant point we are going to make than we do listening to the other person's possible legitimate points and trying to find some areas of agreement and understanding. A great place to see this in action is in interviews with politicians, especially congressmen at the national level! It's even better if they have two opposing sides in the same interview.

What about people we really just plain don't like? There may be many reasons we don't like a person. But regardless of the reasons, do we listen well to people we don't care for?

And the list goes on and on. We talk too much and we listen too little. We air our own opinions and find no pleasure in understanding. We feel wise about the things we have said while looking like fools to those around us. Sometimes our foolishness has real consequences that cause us and others real pain, and all because we couldn't keep our mouth shut!

Fools mock at making amends for sin, but goodwill is found among the upright—14:9

I like this one if only because it is all about admitting we are wrong and then doing something concrete about it. The first step is even acknowledging our sin at all. Whether you view that from a spiritual point of view or just an interpersonal one, we all do things that at least complicate the lives of others and at worst cause significant harm. But we sure have trouble seeing and admitting our mistakes. It's so much easier to find blame in the other person or justify why what we did was not really that bad.

According to this proverb, the upright must be those who see their own sin (not the sin of others) and who "clean up their own messes." Maybe it is as simple as an apology. Maybe there is some action that is needed to make amends. This is hard enough to do with people we like and care about. It's really challenging when those we sin against are people we don't like! After all, they had it coming!

How are we doing cleaning up the messes we make?

It is to a man's honor to avoid strife, but every fool is quick to quarrel—20:2

A fool gives full vent to his anger, but a wise man keeps himself under control—29:11

It seems to me that many people not only enjoy conflict but actively seek it out (remember my soccer club meeting?). These angry, argumentative individuals are thorns in many of our sides. We see them coming and we run the other way. We intentionally avoid situations and events where we know they will be present. And we easily find others who feel the same way about these individuals, confirming that our judgment is correct.

But of course, these proverbs aren't about other people, at least not until we apply them to ourselves! Emotional control and managing relational conflict are difficult matters and they are often related to the fool's good idea that what I think is right because I think it. I know that I have more often than I would care to admit found myself releasing emotion during conflict for personal gratification even with close family members mostly because I didn't want to avoid it. It is a pretty ugly situation and the only solution is to admit that I am a fool!

A man's folly ruins his life, yet his heart rages against the Lord—19:2

"Why me, God? How could you do this to me? What did I do to deserve this?" So many of us are secretly and sometimes not so secretly angry at God for not meeting our expectations. So many of us would be in a much better position if we could see how we got into bad situations in the first place! To be clear, this proverb is not applicable in health situations in which a person is suddenly stricken with a disease that is not and was not preventable. Automobile accidents and their ilk are also not included. However, when the accident is caused by bad judgment, say drinking and driving or as we experienced at one of my schools this year, inexperienced driving in conditions where the individual should not have been driving at all but was doing so anyway, there is folly involved that God had nothing to do with. When the health problem is related to years of poor habits, say smoking or eating poorly, individual folly has to be considered.

Many if not most of us will not have to deal with major events in the lives of our immediate families that have no clear connection with some level of folly. However, if we are able to be honest, many of the problems we experience in our lives can be traced to folly, much of it of our own doing. How easy is it to embrace our folly and take responsibility for the consequences? Doing so ends up being the only way not to be a long-term fool!

As a dog returns to its vomit, so a fool repeats his folly.—26:11

Enough said? Probably! We are good not only at being fools but at proving it again and again!

There are many other proverbs both from the bible book of Proverbs and from other sources of knowledge and insight. No one is going to be hurt by looking into the biblical proverbs even if you don't believe the bible in any other area. They have some great wisdom and are especially valuable when one looks at how they apply to oneself rather than going for the natural tendency to read a really good proverb and think, "Bob could really use this one!" Reading these proverbs and others like them can be very useful in keeping us off the fool's road or at least recognizing that we are on it sooner so we can turn around!

You Are Going to Be Some Kind of Fool!

As we come to the end, it is fitting to reach this conclusion—you are going to be a fool and there is nothing you can do about it! This may be a bit odd since we have been talking about fool's good and real good and presumably trying to choose the latter! But with the way that the world and human relationships actually work, you are going to be somebody's fool!

And here is why: Unless you are a hermit living in a cave with no human contact, everything in your life is being viewed by an audience. And that audience made up of other people who know you and see you and listen to you and have very real opinions about what they know and see and hear. And in the audience of your life, there are differing opinions about what is foolish and what is not. You are going to be some kind of fool—and this is good news!

It would be wonderful to live in a world where everyone could do as he or she wished and no one would ever judge or condemn or call anyone else a fool. Wouldn't that be great? Can't we all just get along? Imagine there's no heaven; it's easy if you try. In that world, it would be possible to live in such a way that you would never be a fool because nothing would be foolish. Cool.

Unfortunately, this is a worldview that simply is not supported by what we witness in the world we actually live in whether we consider our individual relationships or look at world events. People do not like each other and judgment and division seem to be the rule. We know what is good and what is evil and quickly identify them both in others we meet. Those who are like us are in, and those who don't are out. One group is made up of our friends; the other group, if we are not careful, become our enemies. Human history seems to bear this out and we see it happening today in places like Libya and Syria and Afghanistan and inner city Chicago and the US/Mexican border and so on. "Nation rising against nation and kingdom against kingdom" (Matthew 24:7).

And if we really did live in a world where everybody could do whatever they wanted and no one could tell them that they were wrong, what would the limits of that be? Does anyone really want that kind of world? Does there not need to be some order? Some boundaries? Is it okay for the guy down the street to keep kicking his dog? Or his wife and kids? Is it okay for the people of Haiti to continue to live in what we in the US would consider inhumane conditions waiting until there is another disaster for people to notice?

As it turns out, it is fortunate that we do **not** live in that kind of world. We live in a world in which even staunch atheists believe in good and bad, right and wrong (Remember the billboard "I can be good without God?"). We may not agree on what is good and evil in every sense, or where good and evil come from, but everyone knows they are out there. In the Genesis worldview, our being formed in the image of God gives us a desire to do good things—to do things right. But the witness of the world around us makes it plain that while we do some things right, as a group we have done a lot of things wrong, too! Why? We are all doing the best we can. We are trying to do good. We have good intentions. In the Genesis story, the "why" comes from humanity taking on what only God has the wisdom to do and that is to define goodness. Even those who do not subscribe to the Big Bite Theory of Genesis are defining goodness every day and in every experience.

And believers and non-believers alike (regardless of what they believe or don't believe!) are defining you! To some of those people in your life, you are going to look like a fool. That's good news! Since you are going to be some kind of fool, why not decide what kind of fool you are going to be? Many people work very hard at never looking foolish in anyone's eyes no matter what. They work hard to always be in control not only of their own behaviors but also in control of what others think about them. This is a fool's errand to be sure!

Instead, why not choose your primary audience and determine not to be a fool in their eyes? Whose approval do you desire the most? Perhaps your spouse or children or parents? Perhaps the people in your church or religious group? Perhaps the guys on your soccer team? Perhaps the voters in your district? The other parents in the playgroup? Your co-workers?

If you step back from the various groups of which you are a member, it is likely that you will see some of them as more good than others. It is also likely that what is good in the eyes of the members of one group is not necessarily the same as it is in the eyes of members of some of the other groups. If you do one thing, you will look great to some folks and like a fool to others. This can drive a person nuts—constantly trying to fit into or at least not stick out in any surrounding. When teenagers do this, we call it peer pressure and we tell them not to do it . . . remember?

But for those who will accept it, this concept of knowing that a person will always look like a fool in someone's eyes is empowering because it gives the individual the right of decision and virtually eliminates the surprise when encountering the judgment of others. You get to decide what kind of fool you are going to be! Or more accurately, you get to decide which kinds of people will think you are a fool. This is very liberating! "I know that people are going to judge me according to their ideas of what is right and wrong and I DON'T CARE! Because I am only concerned about what this group or individual thinks. I don't want to be a fool in their eyes. If that means that everyone else on earth thinks I am a fool, then so be it!"

As a word of warning or perhaps clarification, this does get us back into the ever-shrinking series of circles. The truth is that eventually everyone you know will think you are a fool at one time or another. They may not use that term, but on some level, that is what they are thinking! This takes us to a discussion about integrity that could occupy another couple of chapters or books. But mostly, it comes down to this: maybe there is only one person in whose eyes you don't want to be a fool—your own. Maybe knowing what you believe and sticking to it no matter what anyone says is the best way to control your own foolishness.

Unfortunately, while this idea has great worldly appeal, it returns us to the trap of thinking that each person can make up their own rights and wrongs and as long as they live those rights and wrongs with integrity, then it is okay that everyone else thinks they are a fool. It also has appeal if we subscribe to the worldview that assumes that people are basically good and left to their own they will come up with reasonable rights and wrongs. As we have talked about in a number of ways, this leaves us with no defensible argument against those who come to the decision that blowing themselves up and taking as many people with them as possible is a "good" thing to do.

So, where are we? We are going to be a fool in someone's eyes no matter what we do. Trying to live in such a way that no one ever thinks we are foolish is a losing proposition. We can try to control our audience and live in such a way that those whose opinions matter to us the most do not think we are fools. This gets us closer to what we are looking for and puts us in control of our foolishness. But we are still in some ways beholden to the opinions and judgments of others. More than that, even those who are closest to us will not always see the great wisdom of our actions or ideas. Even they will think we are fools sometimes.

That leaves us alone with the mirror. So we purpose in our minds that we will live up to our own strongly held convictions no matter what anyone says. We will be our own person and not let others decide for us what is right and what is wrong. We will resist peer pressure!

But how can we know we are really good? How can we know that our thoughts and ideas and opinions are really right and those who think differently are really wrong? It seems so obvious that others are wrong! But if we can step back from ourselves for a minute, we see that there are people on the other side of the opinion who are also alone with their mirrors and who have also purposed that they are going to do what they think is right no matter what anyone says. That person is just like me, but they came to a different conclusion. Who's right? More than that, there is this nagging voice in our conscience questioning the assumption of our own inherent goodness in the first place.

There seem to be only two basic categories to resolve this issue. One comes from the prevalent worldview that people are basically good and that everyone's opinion is of equal value in the economy of right and wrong. This is fool's good and leads to chaos in individual, family, community, and world relationships. It has a broad surface appeal but it proves to be of little value in addressing real conflict. Everyone is right so no one is wrong and we are back to the beginning of the problem.

The second category to resolve the issue of who is right involves recognizing and seeking after an objective source of right and wrong by which all opinions can be measured. In the Genesis worldview, this objective source of right and wrong is, of course, God. But even if you are not there in terms of believing in the God of Genesis, I hope that you will consider the need we as humans have for there to be some Truth by which all truths can be measured. This is a much messier affair than the simple approach that all opinions are right and that no one can tell anyone else that they are right or wrong. Thinking according to standards or *A* standard means mining deeply into human experience corporately and personally to discover the intricacies of that standard. But it is in this experience that real value—real "gold"—is discovered as well.

This second way of resolving the issue also means comparing oneself to that one standard. In that comparison we invariably must face the truth that regardless of our strongly held opinions and feelings related to a subject, *we might be wrong*. This is also a very difficult process. Because if we honestly discover that we are wrong, we must then change our opinions to match the Truth. It is a refining process in which the waste material surrounding the real gold is removed. In refining of gold, this is done physically, chemically, and with heat. If gold had feelings, it would no doubt say, "Hey, this hurts!" Gold does not have feelings, but we do. And if we begin to recognize that there is a standard, we will encounter some discomfort as we compare ourselves to that standard. We will have to strip away some of the garbage with which we have surrounded the core of gold that has been placed in every human being.

People are not good. But they are the most valuable thing that exists. There is nothing more precious than a single human life. But that value does not come from the inherent goodness of the person. If the level of individual human goodness determined the value of a person, some people would be more valuable than others based on the goodness as perceived by others. We have certainly experimented with that idea in human history. Slavery is the best example. And slavery is not just a part of human history but human trafficking continues today as horrific as ever. Would anyone want to argue that the life of a young woman trapped in a world of sexual slavery is less valuable than say, my own 17-year-old daughter? Would anyone want to argue that the people who enslave others are entitled to their opinions of what is right and wrong in the treatment of others and therefore it is okay for them to practice and profit from human trafficking?

Human value does not come from the goodness of a person, but because a person has inherent worth in spite of their badness. In the Genesis worldview, this is played out in the New Testament with the sacrifice of Jesus for all people. Paul puts this in economic terms saying, "You are not your own, you were bought at a price." (1 Corinthians 6:19) While this may sound like the slavery we just rejected above, the price that was paid was paid in order to redeem people from the slavery in which they found themselves. It was paid to set them free, not to put them in bondage. It was paid to show just how much God thinks human life is worth. It was paid as a way to refine the gold in each person and to purify them to the state of true value for which they were created.

And in the Genesis worldview, it was paid as a demonstration of the standard to which all human lives will be compared. A while back, there was the WWJD craze, "What Would Jesus Do?" It was well intentioned and spoke about the standard of comparison that we are considering. But as the WWJD letters became a part of our American culture, it was interesting to see people from various groups and viewpoints using the WWJD letters to back up their opinions. You could figuratively see people on both sides of a street shouting at each other about some issue or another, both with signs asking WWJD? Both sides seemed to believe that if Jesus were present, he would be on their side of the street! This is not what we are talking about here. Taking Jesus, or any other figure, religious or otherwise, and dragging that figure into the discussion on your side is not comparing oneself to a standard. That's just another way of saying that I AM the standard!

Perhaps a better process is to start with the standard and then ask this question, first of myself, and then of any groups or causes to which I belong: "Am I right or am I wrong?" And to ask that question genuinely looking for problems not in the standard, but in my thinking. The foundational idea is that if there is a difference between the standard and my thoughts, the problem always lies with me. The opposite of this is seen in statements made by many people along the lines of "I could never believe in a god who (fill in the blank)." In this way of thinking, if there is a god and he doesn't agree with me then he is wrong! There is no attempt to seek truth through self-examination.

Certainly, we can understand the difficulties many people have in understanding and accepting a god or a standard. We can't know the background that leads people to think the way they do. People have had all manner of pain and brokenness in their lives and we may not be privy to any of it. But pain and brokenness do not by their existence negate the possibility of a standard. And that standard may be the only key to healing because a standard gives order to a universe that for some people has truly been unpredictable, unreliable, and chaotic. But in order for the standard to be useful for any of us, we have to start with an attitude that says, "I will change to meet the standard instead of changing the standard to meet me."

In 1 Corinthians (4:10), Paul talks about being "fools for Christ." And in his letter to the Philippian church, Paul talks about giving up all things for the sake of Christ. He refers to everything else as "rubbish" (Phil 3:9), or at least that's the NIV translation. The original Greek is apparently a bit more colorful in its description and could be translated as a word not typically used in polite company. But that's what Paul had come to believe about his own righteousness. It simply had no value worth having. He wanted the standard and was willing to do whatever it took to get to the standard even if everyone else thought him a fool. He wanted real good, not fool's good.

What would the world be like if everyone took this approach? To spend much more time assessing one's own comparison with the standard rather than quickly defaulting to easy to come by judgments about where others fall short. To get the whole world to do this may be a stretch. But a few people can start the process and indeed many already have. The result may just be a slightly better family, neighborhood, church, soccer team, volunteer group, community, etc. No more fool's gold. Only the real thing for us from now on. More work, sure. But more reward as well. What kind of fool will you be?

About the Author

Jim Ott has been serving children in schools as a school psychologist in Eastern Iowa since 1984. He has also been involved in youth and camp ministry for more than 20 years locally and on a state level. More recently, he has been involved in establishing a community empowering program in his home town of Dubuque that is addressing poverty through education and relationships across class lines. He has been a member of First Baptist Church of Dubuque for more than 25 years where he currently serves as worship leader and Sunday School teacher.

Jim has been married to Teresa since 1984 and they have four children who are doing many wonderful things. Jim has a passion for helping others realize their true value and overcome barriers. And he loves to make children laugh.

Jim is a dynamic speaker who is well-known for engaging his audiences in thought-provoking discussions, workshops, and seminars. Send an email to jmott30@aol.com to schedule a speaking engagement.